# TREASURES OF DORSET

Jean Bellamy

With Illustrations by Judith Fry

*Front cover:* Upwey Church

Published by
Thornhill Press
24 Moorend Road
Cheltenham
MCMXCI

ISBN 0 946328 36 6

Jean Bellamy [©]

Drawings by Judith Fry [©]

Typeset in Times 10/12
Printed by View Publications (Bristol) Ltd., Wickwar, Glos.

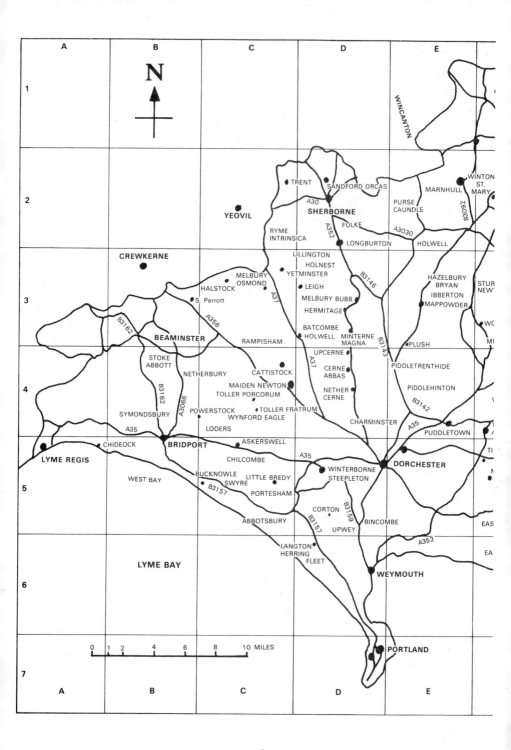

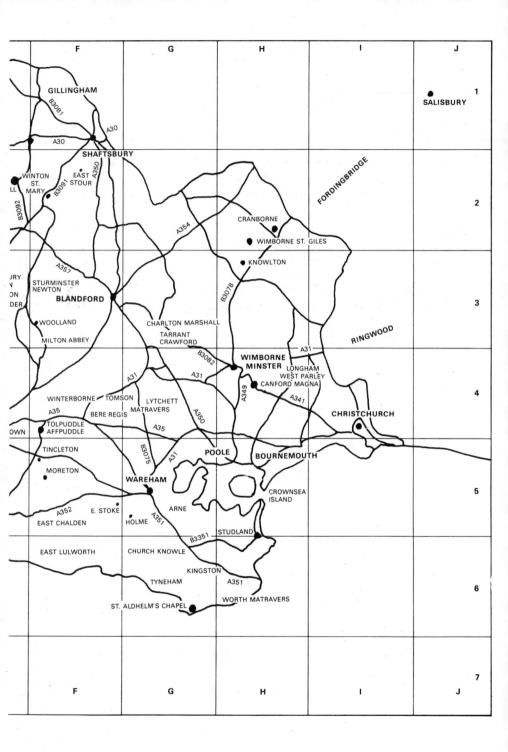

# INTRODUCTION

The purpose of this book is to highlight, with the aid of photographs and line drawings, the attractions of a selection of Dorset villages, with particular emphasis on the county's many historic churches.

# ACKNOWLEDGEMENTS

My thanks are due to the Editor of 'DORSET LIFE', for allowing me to draw upon information from articles of mine that have appeared in the magazine.

# CONTENTS

# ABBOTSBURY

Large and picturesque, its houses and cottages of yellow-brown stone mostly thatched, Abbotsbury became important in ancient times largely due to its association with the Benedictine monastery of St. Peter founded 900 years ago during the reign of King Canute.

During the Middle Ages the village achieved great fame, but with the dissolution of the monasteries, most of its monastic buildings disappeared – with the exception of the 14th century chapel of St. Catherine, perched on an elevation atop a conical hill. Perhaps it survived because it lay at a distance, or perhaps it was just too massive to destroy. At any rate, whatever the cause, it still stands.

A walk up the steep, 250-foot hill grazed by hundreds of sheep is rewarding. Like its namesake at St. Aldhelm's Head in the Purbecks, set bleakly on a headland and exposed to all winds and weathers, the little building is a wishing chapel. Its age is not known exactly, though it is older than the church of St. Nicholas, but not as old as the Tithe Barn. Measuring 45' x 15' inside, with 4-foot thick walls, an octagonal tower, two porches and heavy buttressing to support the great weight of the barrel roof, it was built to last. For four to five hundred years it has acted as a look-out and beacon.

Yet it is for its massive tithe barn that the village is famous. Once forming part of the monastery, this impressive building of buttressed stone, 272' long by 31' wide, was erected about 500 years ago. Originally used as a grain-store and for shearing sheep, it is now in ruins for half its length. Today it houses the locally-grown reeds used in the thatching of cottage roofs, for which reason it is not normally open to the public.

A Saxon church had existed in Abbotsbury in olden times, although it was the Abbey that was of prime importance. On the break up of the monastery, the land passed to Sir Giles Strangways, and has been held by his descendents, the Earls of Ilchester, ever since. The manor house, of which all that remains today is the arch standing close to the church, was built out of the Abbey ruins and was the home of the Fox-Strangways. It is due to this family retaining and administering the lands down to the present time that the village has remained so well-preserved.

The church of St. Nicholas is largely 15th century and possesses an early Jacobean or late Tudor pulpit, panelled and with a high back and sounding board. Worth noting are the two holes in the pulpit's canopy, made by the bullets of Cromwell's men when church and nearby manor were garrisoned for Charles during the Civil War. An extract from a contemporary account of the attack by Sir Ashley Cooper on 8th November 1644 still exists. 'After a hot bickering,' it runs, 'the church was carried and all 13 defenders taken. The manor was blown up and all within it perished'. When the timbers of the north aisle were being removed during the renovation of 1930, yet two more bullet holes were discovered. Located in one of the beams of the aisle roof, the flattened-out bullets were found to be still fixed inside.

Popular with Abbotsbury's summer visitors are its gardens, first planted in the 18th century, and its world-famous Swannery. Partly natural and partly man-made, the latter is 600 years old, has an ancient duck decoy, and is set amidst surroundings which have changed little since before 1400. Nestling on the shores of the Fleet, the Swannery is separated from the sea by 9 miles of the Chesil beach. An area of great natural beauty, it teems with wild life, including one thousand mute swans and their cygnets, the only colony in the world which is open to visitors during nesting time. Covering 25 acres, it claims to be the biggest sanctuary in the country, and is mentioned in Queen Elizabeth I's confirmation of her father's grant of the Manor to the Fox-Strangways.

# ASKERSWELL

This village lies deep in a valley beneath the dual carriageway between Dorchester and Bridport. The approach is steep and by way of narrow lanes. Scattered due to its varying levels, Askerswell contains some interesting buildings, including the Granary and the mellow Old School House standing on rising ground.

Prominently sited is the church of St. Michael, though due to rebuilding in 1858 the 15th century tower is the only original part remaining. Against a wall of the nave may be seen what is believed to be an ancient sepulchral stone. Of date 1320, this slab is of the same dimensions and material and the lettering of the same type as that of another monumental stone to be found in the church of St. Candida, Whitchurch Canonicorum. Because of the many years of traffic passing over the latter, the wording is much worn and almost illegible; though if the two slabs were to be placed side by side, part of the inscription would read: 'Sir Thomas de Luda and Lady Alianore, his wife, lie here'. It is clear that the slabs at one time formed the covering of the same tomb, but how they came to be sited in two different churches is a matter for speculation.

To the north of Askerswell, Eggardon Hill rises to a height of 800 feet and commands magnificent views to south and east.

Askerswell

# BATCOMBE

The population of this remote village has dwindled over the years and today it comprises only a few cottages and a farmhouse. Batcombe Hill under which it lies is steep and narrow and leads down to the church of St. Mary Magdalen, battlemented and of Ham Hill stone and flint. This 15th century building possesses a tower and a stone rood screen of the same date, a 12th century font, and an ancient pillar piscina. Restored in 1864, it still retains its ancient timber roof.

The local legend has been told many times. A 17th century squire, Conjuror Minterne by name, leapt his horse from the side of the steep hill straight over the church tower, knocking off one of the pinnacles in the process. Less familiar are the instructions he is said to have left regarding his burial – half inside, half outside the church. The problem was resolved by burying him below a wall. In 'Tess of the D'Urbervilles' Thomas Hardy refers to him as 'a homely quack called in by farmers when beasts were ill'.

On the top of an adjacent hill exists the mysterious stone known as the Cross-in-hand. Its history, whether Christian or Pagan, is unknown, but it could have been placed there as a boundary mark. This ancient pillar with a top like a clenched fist also features in Hardy's 'Tess'. When she questioned the shepherd as to its meaning, he told her, 'Tis a thing of ill omen, Miss'. Gipsies consider it to be a wishing stone.

Nearby at Hillfield exists the Anglican Friary of St. Francis.

Batcombe

# BERE REGIS

The village of Bere Regis, situated on a southward-flowing chalk stream, stands at the apex of the heath to which it gives its name. An important mediaeval centre, it had associations with King John, who almost certainly hunted there when it was a royal demesne. The King, having abandoned an invasion of Normandy in 1205, landed at Studland and came to Bere Regis. Here he built himself a palace in a field opposite the east end of the church, where now stands Crown Court.

If the village itself is a little disappointing nowadays, the church of St. John the Baptist is said to be one of the loveliest in the country. It contains much of interest, including the man with the toothache clutching his jaw, and the man with the headache grasping his forehead. These are carved on the arches cut into the south wall of the nave and are apparently intended as a warning against the deadly sins of gluttony and drunkenness. Such afflictions must have presented a major problem to those living in the Middle Ages and similar carvings are to be seen at other churches, including Cerne Abbas.

Bere Regis

An entry in the churchwardens' accounts for the year 1738 states: 'Paid Benjamin Moores for Cleaning & Oyling the Apostles . . 4s. 0d.'

Twelve almost life size figures project from the trusses on either side of the magnificent carved and painted oak roof. These were given by Cardinal Morton, Henry VIII's chancellor, who was born in the parish of Milborne St. Andrew. A theory exists that they are in alphabetical order, starting with Andrew on the northern side and finishing up with Thomas on the south. This would seem to be confirmed by the fact that there is a resemblance between the third and fifth figures, the brothers James and John. It will be noticed that John and Matthew, the two Gospel writers, are each holding a book.

In the south aisle are situated the Turberville monuments; though for most people, the name Turberville will bring to mind Thomas Hardy's legendary Tess of the D'Urbervilles, rather than the Turberville family who actually existed.

Outside this remarkable old church which is mentioned in the Domesday Book, lies a peaceful churchyard containing a number of yew trees.

Bere Regis

# BINCOMBE

Above this village near Upwey lies the ancient burial ground of Bincombe Down, popularly known as 'Bincombe Bumps'. From here, Arthur Mee tells us, 'men kept watch over land and sea in the times before our island history had begun'. Today, from the top of Bincombe Hill, the panoramic view includes Portland, the whole of Weymouth Bay, and the coastline stretching far from east to west.

Before the Norman Conquest, 'Beincombe' belonged to Earl Harold; after which, William the Conqueror gave it to the monastery of St. Stephen of Caen. Much later it contained a large encampment of soldiers, mainly regiments of the German Legion. In his 'Trumpet Major', Thomas Hardy describes the excitement amongst the villagers for miles around when, during the Napoleonic wars, soldiers came riding up to the downs with their 'buckles and chains shining like glass, no weather stains to spoil their blue and white uniforms'. Was it here that the Grand old Duke of York marched his ten thousand men up and down the hill?

Bincombe also has connections with Hardy's 'The Melancholy Hussar', of which it formed the background. The story is based on fact, for one of the regiments, the York Hussars, contained two young German mercenaries who deserted. Subsequently caught and accused of spying, they were tried and shot at the crossroads. The earliest church register dates from 1658, and an entry for the year 1801 includes their names. They are believed to be buried in the churchyard beneath two flat, nameless grave-stones lying side by side.

Picturesque, in spite of most of its thatch having disappeared, parts of Bincombe have stood for 800 years. In 1570 the village was bought by Gonville and Caius College, Cambridge, the latter still owning it and being patron of the living. Comprising one or two farms, a handful of cottages, and the little church of Holy Trinity, it lies within a short distance of the main road, though it could be a hundred miles away. Its population has shrunk by half since 1870.

The church is squat towered, in the Early English style of c.1250-1350. Features of particular interest include earlier Norman work to be seen in the blocked up north doorway and the font, the latter bearing traces of the fittings of a former cover. There is a blocked up hagioscope (squint) in the north wall, and a blocked up window high in the south wall is visible from the outside. The windows are of the mid-1400s; the chancel arch was restored in 1862, at which time the chancel was lengthened and the floor raised.

Since 1808 when the Rectory was burnt down, the rector has lived at Broadway. The united parish of Bincombe with Broadway has been united with Upwey and Buckland Ripers since 1981.

Church Porch. Bincombe

# CATTISTOCK

A village of thatch, stone and brick, Cattistock derives its name from the old English 'Catt' – a wild cat, and 'stoc' meaning the place of a religious foundation. Ancient earth works are to be found in the vicinity.

Cattistock

The church of Ss. Peter and Paul was built in 1857 by Sir Gilbert Scott, its most striking feature being its tall, slim tower of grey stone added by his son, George Scott, in 1874. Apparently inspired by that of Charminster church, near Dorchester, it at one time featured a gigantic clock face. It also housed a very fine carillon of thirty-five bells, the melodious tones of which were said to attract folk from far and wide. Unfortunately the peal was destroyed by a fire in the tower during the war (not due to enemy action), and was replaced by a modern one of eight bells.

A church is believed to have existed here in Saxon times; King Alfred's grandson, Athelstan, gave land at Cattistock to the monks at Milton Abbas 18 miles distant. The present building is sombre and contains a tall wooden font cover in the shape of a spire. Situated in a chapel under the tower decorated in dark greens and reds, it rises to an extraordinary height of 20 feet, almost touching the roof. According to Hutchins, the west end of the church and tower were ivy-covered ruins in the 18th century.

Chantmarle House, though included in the parish, is actually situated on the edge of Frome St. Quintin lying a mile or two to the north. Built in 1612 in Tudor style and designed by Sir John Strode of Parnham, it was originally E-shaped, though the wings no longer exist. At one time the headquarters of the Ashdene Press, it later became a police training college.

Cattistock is noted for its Hunt which comprises one of the leading packs in the West Country.

*Cottages at Cattistock*

# CHARMINSTER

Described by Sir Arthur Mee as 'rambling about by the River Cerne, its proud possessions the great house and the church', this village lies close to Dorchester. Dominated by the striking, early 16th century tower of St Mary's, it possesses a 12th century church with a Norman chancel arch. The porch is 700 years old, the wooden pulpit the remains of an old three-decker. Spread around the 15th century tower is a curious double 'T' – a reminder that it was built by Sir Thomas Trenchard of nearby Wolfeton Manor situated in the meadows where the Cerne joins the Frome.

ST MARY THE VIRGIN CHARMINSTER.

Wolfeton House was once the ancient mediaeval seat of the Jurdains and the de Mohuns. From 1480 it was owned by the Trenchards who came from Hordle in Hampshire. Unoccupied by the family for long periods, it fell into disrepair towards the end of the 18th century, but was saved from complete ruin on being bought by a kinsman. In later years, a member of the Bankes family of Kingston Lacy went to live there, and for the last twenty years it has been in the ownership of Captain and Mrs N.T.L. Thimbleby.

This 'romantic fragment of a Tudor house' to which Sir Walter Raleigh was a frequent visitor from Sherborne, is a magnificent stately home, built during the reign of Henry VII. Remodelled in the time of James I, its name is

Saxon in origin, so it is thought likely that an earlier house once occupied the site. With its adjacent farm, it stands amongst the trees, splendid and aloof. Two massive towers of the gatehouse, unequal in size and probably dating from the 14th century, would appear to be the oldest parts remaining. In recent years, clearance of the ivy-covered walls has further enhanced the house, revealing the great beauty of its stonework.

# CHIDEOCK

Between the hills on the Bridport to Lyme Regis road lies Chideock (pronounced 'Chiddick') with its houses of local sandstone and some thatch though, due to the busy main road bisecting it, it is no longer the 'unspoiled old-world village' to which Sir Frederick Treves refers in his 'Highways and Byways of Dorset'. Conspicuous in the vicinity is Moore's Dorset Biscuit factory, noted for its 'Dorset knobs'.

The nave of the parish church of St. Giles dates from the 13th century though the building underwent considerable restoration during Victorian times. A feature of interest is the Arundell Chapel situated in the south aisle, this family being lords of the manor of Chideock from 1450. Two old paintings on the north wall of the nave depict the church as it appeared in the 1800's; and a church leaflet tells of the oldest of the peal of five bells in the belfry which bears the inscription 'Love Dog' – an error occasioned by the accidental transposition of letters during casting in 1602.

Mention of Chideock would not be complete without reference to the 'Chideock Gang', a group of 18th century smugglers who had their lookout post at the top of Golden Cap, the highest point on this part of the coast. Operating under the leadership of a local personality calling himself 'The Colonel', they carried out their activities between Seatown and Charmouth.

In the vicinity exists the site of Stanton St. Gabriel, which lay in the shadow of Golden Cap. To quote Treves again, it was 'a village lost and forgotten centuries ago . . . on a level mead between a wood and the blue waters of Charmouth Bay'. The ruins of the church are still there today.

To the west of Seatown, lying half-a-mile due south of Chideock, Golden Cap rises to a height of 617 feet. Green sand and limestone rock and clay are said to account for the unusual colourings; when the sun shines the cap appears bright gold.

Chideock.

# CHILCOMBE

A mile or so to the north-west of Puncknowle and Swyre lies Chilcombe, tucked well out of sight. Access is via a road crossing the river Bride and later joining the dual carriageway. Just past Rudge Farm, a notice states that access to Chilcombe church lies 300 yards ahead to the right. There is parking for cars in the field, and beyond a gate are grouped a large, late 16th century stone farmhouse once the manor, farm outbuildings, and a little 13th century church with neither spire nor tower.

Of unknown dedication, the church occupies a tiny churchyard – surely one of the smallest in existence – comprising a few graves beneath a yew tree. A bantam or two, plus a hen and her chicks were the only signs of life on the occusion of my visit. Apart from the intermittent crowing of a cockerel, the silence was complete.

The church's seating capacity is forty. It contains a 12th century font with cable moulding, a Norman arch, and some 15th century stained glass. In the chancel, an armchair of the Bishop family bears the carved initials, 'R.B. 1642', and is thought to have stood in the same position for almost 3½ centuries. A member of this family built the adjacent manor house in 1578 and later the estate passed to Lord Nelson's family. Like many other Dorset parishes, Chilcombe was deprived of its clergy during the Black Death.

Perhaps the most interesting feature of the church is the curious panel, engraved and inlaid, which portrays scenes from the Crucifixion. Of Elizabethan date and foreign, it was used for some time as a reredos, and is believed to have been a spoil of the Armada.

Chilcombe.

# CHURCH KNOWLE

Situated two to three miles westward of Corfe, this pretty little village consists of grey stone cottages, a small post office, a general store and a pub.

The church of St. Peter is thirteenth century, though the tower was rebuilt in 1741. A list of rectors dates back to 1327, and the church registers, which are now lodged with the County Archivist at Dorchester, go back to 1548. Interestingly, they contain records of those who, between the years 1685 and 1789, were buried in wool in order to stimulate the woollen industry. This strange custom was compulsory for a period of 120 years.

In the idyllic surroundings of Church Knowle exists an Animal Sanctuary which attracts numerous visitors during the summer months. Of 25 years' standing, it celebrated its Silver Jubilee last year.

Church Knowle

# CORTON

Corton Farm and its ancient chapel lie off the Portesham/Upwey Road, at the bottom of a steep incline. The turning is signposted but could easily be missed, so visitors to this tranquil spot are few. The chapel, its grey-green, lichen-covered walls blending perfectly with its surroundings, nestles against the hillside. The lovely old manor farmhouse is situated just below.

This is a chantry chapel dedicated to St. Bartholomew; it has stood here since the 15th century. As one enters through the small arched doorway, there is a sense of timelessness – a link with an age long gone. The interior is neat and well-kept, the font, lectern and wooden pews well proportioned for the size of the building.

The chapel's most stiking feature is the simple stone altar. Almost certainly one of a very few now remaining, it is typical of its kind – a long flat slab supported at either end by two stone uprights. On top of the slab may be seen the outlines of three crosses of which there were originally five.

In the Domesday Book, the chantry chapel is referred to as 'Corfeton', meaning a 'town of the gap'. At that time, it was worth £7 and was owned by one Roger de Curcelle. Subsequent to the passing of the Chantry Act in 1552, it ceased to be used for religious purposes, but became a part of the farm buildings. Outhouses were added at either end and carpentry work took place in its interior. It also came into use as a wheelwright's shop, and at a later stage housed horses and poultry.

Yet during those years, the ancient stone altar remained intact and undisturbed. Thus it came about that a description of this interesting little building was given to the Diocese – as a result of which it was decided to restore it for use as a church again. £250 was the target for re-roofing and conversion into a mission church for the poor of the neighbourhood. Money was raised for the removal of the farm sheds and re-erection elsewhere, as well as for new fittings for the chapel. The sum required was raised in 1897 and the little chantry was re-dedicated that same year, the ceremony being performed by the Lord Bishop of Salisbury.

Information taken from ancient documents and newspaper cuttings has revealed some interesting facts about the chantry. The stone altar dates from certainly not later than 1400; though an 'arca' or altar of three slabs speaks of the highest antiquity, so that it probably dates from very early English. In addition, it is of Purbeck marble which was highly thought of in those times, as well as during the Norman and Saxon period.

The 'fair house' below, once the manse, is a substantial building with flat-topped and arched windows. Originally extending as far as the wall fronting the terrace, it has been shortened by about one-third of its length and enjoys extensive and uninterrupted views across open fields. In 1381, the manor house was acknowledged a rectory chantry and valued at £4.10s 0d. It was subsequently held for several generations by the Courtenay family (Earls of Devonshire), during which time the daughter married Maximillian Mohun, this family having connections with nearby Fleet. They lost it in the Civil War, however, and after that it changed hands several times.

Beyond Corton, the narrow winding road, marred only by pylons, continues on in the direction of Portesham. The countryside becomes increasingly hilly, and Jacob sheep (belonging to Corton Farm) are frequently in evidence on the slopes.

Corton

# EAST CHALDON

The pretty village of East Chaldon (or Chaldon Herring) lies remote amongst the downs nine miles west of Wareham. To the rear and above rises the ridge known as Fossil Hill, from which marvellous views of the surrounding countryside are obtainable. Here is a series of rounded barrows known as the Five Marys (or Meers), in one of which a 19th century excavation revealed skeletons of a man and woman with stags's antlers on their shoulders; in another, a man on his own also with antlers.

The well-kept church of St. Nicholas, stands in a peaceful setting by roadside. Norman in origin and with an ancient font, it was restored in the 15th century and again in 1879. The Communion Table, pulpit and lectern were made by a Canon of Upwey with his own hands. Of particular interest is the picture designed in 1940 by Elizabeth Muntz, the sculptress. Cut-out figures of animals representing local characters were stitched in place by the children of the village. In the background are the tumuli already mentioned, the Five Marys. In the well-tended churchyard may be seen Elizabeth Muntz's tombstone, designed by herself before her death.

At intervals along the nearby cliffs are three marker stones in the form of sculptured whelk shells standing in stone niches, each set at a different angle. They are monuments to the three Powys brothers – John Cowper Powys, novelist; A.R. Powys, architect and secretary to the Society for the Protection of Ancient Buildings; and T.F. Powys, novelist, who lived in East Chaldon in a small red Victorian house called 'Beth Car'. In his masterpiece, 'Mr. Weston's Good Wine', T.F. Powys described the village under the name of Folly Down. Between village and sea, a memorial stone is to Llewellyn Powys. It bears the dates '13th Aug 1884 to 2nd Dec 1939' and the words, 'The Living. The Living. He shall praise Thee'.

East Chaldon's inn, The Sailor's Return, is neatly-thatched and recently extended. It provides a good meal.

Cottages at East Chaldon

# EAST and WEST HOLME

Tucked away just south of the main road from Wool to Wareham lie the little village of East Holme, the hamlet known as West Holme, and the village of East Stoke. Possibly due to the fact that there is little to attract tourists to this particular area (except on the occasions when Tyneham and Worbarrow Bay are open to the public) it has remained unspoilt and uninvaded by sightseers.

Bindon Lane, along with Holme Lane which is a continuation of it, could probably qualify as amongst the prettiest roads in Dorset – and this in spite of the Army occupying the territory immediately to the south and as far as the coast.

It is thought that the names Holme Lane, East Holme and West Holme may have derived from the old word for 'holly'. Certainly this plant is in evidence, along with beeches, firs, oaks, and in early Summer masses of magnificent rhododendrons. This is a delightful spot, with the Purbeck Hills visible to the south and the lanes banked high with greenery and splashes of wonderful purple blooms. As one follows their twists and turns, sometimes beneath a thick canopy of leaves where the trees meet overhead, one is grateful that, unlike many another route, they have remained unwidened and unaltered.

At West Holme exist a manor house, cottages, and an observatory tower. Turning off to East Holme, one comes upon some fine parkland with trees and meadows and a Georgian house – all within a short distance of the Army ranges. The house possesses a 16th century Elizabethan core, and the south front and park date from 1770. Considerable alteration was carried out in 1830.

The Manor House West Holme

29

Adjacent to the house stands the small church of St. John the Evangelist, Early English in style and still with its original nave, chancel, vestry and bell-cote. Built in 1866 by Nathaniel Bond of Holme Priory, and his wife, Lady Selina Bond, Purbeck marble was used in its construction, along with local stone. The church was positioned so as to avoid low ground and waterlogging, as also the burial ground to preclude contamination of wells in the area.

A Cluniac foundation of 1107, East Holme Priory was founded in 1142 by Robert de Lincoln who held Wareham Castle for Queen Matilda. It was a cell of Montacute Priory in Somerset and occupied a site to the rear of the present house. With never more than twelve monks in occupation, at the Dissolution of 1535 only two remained. Stone from the old priory was used in the building of the church, and also of the ornate Norman arches of the 18th century chapel at Creech Grange.

Leaving East Holme, one is confronted by a water-splash and a warning to check ones brakes. Beyond, one arrives at the main road via an automatic level-crossing, passing en route Holme-bridge which is really two bridges – one old and of brick-and-flint, the other modern. Here, during the Civil War, Royalists held the crossing against Parliamentarian forces and overcame them.

East Holme.

# FLEET

There is a slightly eerie quality about the still, silent, inland stretch of sea known as the Fleet, particularly on a cloudy day. A strange, tidal salt water lake eight miles long and extending from Abbotsbury to Portland, it is shallow, weed-filled and stony, the haunt of an abundance of diving and wading birds. Fishermen use flat-bottomed boats from which to catch eels, bass and mullet, though no other type of boat is to be seen and it is unsuitable for swimming. Swans abound in this lonely spot, flying backwards and forwards between the lake and Abbotsbury's famous Swannery.

It was on the ancient, now almost non-existent village of East Fleet that Meade Falkner based his well-known novel, 'Moonfleet'. During the great storm of 1824, when a 95-ton ship was hurled up over the Chesil Bank, the village was almost totally destroyed. Only six cottages survived, of which five were wiped out by fire in 1938, but have since been rebuilt.

All but the chancel of the little parish church was swept away in the storm. Situated beyond the row of cottages, most of which were once thatched, the tiny chancel has been well-preserved and is worth a visit. Inside may be seen three tablets to the Mohuns, the two dated 1603 and 1612 having brasses depicting fourteen sons and sixteen daughters, children of the two couples commemorated. There is said to be an underground passageway beneath the chancel, once used by smugglers.

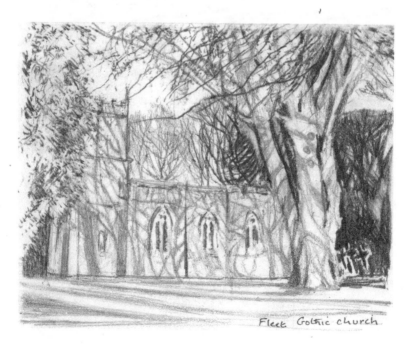

Fleet Gothic church

31

Since the 16th century, Fleet had connections with the Mohun family of Fleet House, until the estate passed by marriage to John Gould of Upwey. One of John's sons, the Reverend George Gould, incumbent of the parish at the time of the disaster of 1824, did much to assist the villagers. The parish church of Holy Trinity, which replaced the former building, was erected at his expense in 1829 and stands amongst beech trees just below the level of the road. The attractive, pinkish tinge of its brickwork is the result of the lichen growing over the smooth ashlar surface. Inside may be seen a memorial to George's brother, John, who died in 1826. A tablet on the wall of the porch commemorates both George Gould and the dedication of the church by the Bishop of Bristol on 25th August 1829.

The Moonfleet Hotel, formerly Fleet House, dates back to 1603 and is a mixture of buildings from the 17th century onwards. Large gate-piers, once carrying the insignia of the lords of the manor, flank the road giving access to this remote village of Fleet.

The chancel of Old Fleet church.

# HALSTOCK

This village lying close to the Somerset/Dorset border, is famous for its inn, The Quiet Woman. Unlike her counterpart at Wareham, she holds her head under her arm, and according to tradition represents a 7th century saint

1991 inn sign
Halstock

named St. Juthware who used to assist pilgrims en route for Halstock's shrine. Her stepmother and brother became angry at this continued stream of visitors to the house, and one day her brother, in a rage, cut off her head with his sword. Whereupon, so legend says, she picked it up and walked with it to the church before finally passing out.

The church of St. Mary was rebuilt in 1845, though the early Perpendicular tower with its weathered gargoyles is of the 15th century. Nave and aisle are by A.W. Pugin.

Two thousand years ago, a fine Roman house seems to have existed at Halstock – for in recent times its mosaic pavement has been unearthed and covered up again. Arthur Mee tells of traces of old pack road, and of field names that seem to hint at buildings long since vanished. He also mentions five bells in the church tower covering the reigns of all the Stuarts – probably cast by the Purdues whose foundary was in Closworth village.

# HERMITAGE

The name of this village is thought to have come from some Augustinian friars who settled here, perhaps during the 12th century, in what was then known as the Forest of Blackmore. Under the direct protection of the King, they received grants of land from Edward II. The name is certainly appropriate, for Hermitage's population is only 80, and it is tucked well away at the foot of High Stoy, a grassy hill rising to a height of 860 feet.

Hermitage.

In later years, when the forest disappeared, the church became a perpetual curacy in the gift of the Duchy of Cornwall. Restored in the 17th century, it was largely rebuilt around 1800, complete with barrel roof and a bell turret; the latter replacing the original tower which, somewhat strangely, contained an apartment for the use of the curate. Over the porch was said to have existed a room which was used for storing wood for his fire.

On 13th January 1583, a curious occurrence was reputed to have taken place in the village. The inhabitants were going about their business as usual when they were terrified almost out of their wits by an earthquake. A three-acre field rose suddenly into the air and was carried bodily over another field to a distance of approximately 300 yards, where it came to rest, completely blocking a road. The cause was a small landslide, but many legends arose as a result.

During the second world war, the Bournemouth Art Gallery hung several of its large pictures inside the church for safe keeping. At the present time, Hermitage is one of five parishes making up the High Stoy group.

# HINTON ST. MARY

There is a fine manor house at Hinton St. Mary, dating from 1649 and occupying the site of a mediaeval monastic building. A mill exists here too – a tranquil spot situated half-a-mile down a quiet lane, on the banks of the Stour. William Barnes, the Dorset poet, lived just across the fields as a child, and would often come here to play.

Hinton St. Mary

Beside the Manor stands the church of St. Peter, elevated and with fine views of Blackmore Vale. Rebuilt in 1846 except for the tower, it possesses a 17th century Freke monument. Thomas Freke, son of Robert Freke and auditor and teller of the Exchequer during the reigns of Henry VIII and Elizabeth, built the adjacent manor house.

From the Frekes, the manor passed by marriage to the Pitts, and thus to General Pitt-Rivers, well-known for his excavations on Romano-British sites. It is interesting that this house, restored by the General's grandson, contains a Tudor ceiling from Fiddleford Mill.

St Peter Hinton St Mary

# HOLWELL

A street of stone cottages, an 18th century rectory, stocks, and a church standing by the Caundle Brook make up this attractive village. The church of St. Lawrence, brown-stoned and with a fine tower, possesses a number of horrific gargoyles. Restored in 1885, it has two original panelled roofs; the one in the nave a barrel roof with a cornice adorned with Tudor roses, the other timber and carved with foliage and stars.

Strongly reminiscent of France are the surroundings of the old Jacobean manor, Holwell House, a mile to the south-west. Three-storeyed and with tall, gabled dormers, it is situated amidst wood and coppice facing an unfenced road. The site is believed to have had connections with King John, an old record stating that the house stood on land occupied by the chief hunting lodge of the Forest of Blackmore. The village was once recorded as being a detached part of Somerset incorporated with Dorset.

Holwell

# KNOWLTON

The deserted village of Knowlton lies to the south of Wimborne St. Giles in the parish of Woodlands and is noted for its ruined church. The name is said to have derived from the Saxon 'Unolle' – 'the top of the hill'. Situated on the west side of the main Wimborne to Cranborne road, the village – once a Royal manor and mentioned in the Domesday Book – stretched along the southern bank of the river Allen, to the south-west of Brockington Farm. This farmstead stands on the remains of another old, but not entirely deserted village thought to have connected at one time with Knowlton.

The ruins of Knowlton church stand in a circular earthwork with two entrances, roughly 300 yards from the lost village. This earthwork – a bank with a ditch about 100 yards across – is a prehistoric 'henge' or ritual monument of the Bronze age, the purpose of which was to protect the outside world from the egress of malignant spirits confined within the church. The building dates from the 12th century and numbers amongst many notable prehistoric monuments in the area. Unlike most parish churches, however, which were originally erected to serve the needs of the local community, the siting of Knowlton church is thought to have had other, more mysterious reasons. It may have been occupied successively by Celt, Roman and Saxon, until the time that Christianity arrived. So it is considered possible that the church within its sacred circle was built for the purpose of exorcising evil powers.

It is believed that four thousand years ago Knowlton may have ranked third to Stonehenge and Avebury in this part of the country as an important religious centre. Worship continued from about 1800 B.C. until the church was abandoned in comparatively recent times. Evidence for the existence of this continuity of worship is said to be stronger here than anywhere else in Dorset.

Knowlton Church.

At one time a chapel of ease to Horton, the church fell into disrepair around the year 1650 and was unused for a considerable time. Somewhere around the year 1735 it was repaired, but unfortunately the roof collapsed soon afterwards and it was never used again. Though considerably enlarged during the 15th century – possibly due to a rise in population – it is still a small church. A record of 1550 tells of a curate named Richard Saunders, in whose time three bells existed in the tower.

The eventual depopulation of the village is believed to have been a result of the plague, which played an important part in the history of some of Dorset's villages. A fair which once existed was eventually moved to nearby Woodlands, where – in the latter's 18th century parish church – stands Knowlton's font.

# LEIGH

Considerable outward extension has taken place in this village lying a mile or so east of Chetnole. Large Ham-stone cottages, many with mullioned windows, intersperse with more modern buildings. A hump-backed bridge crosses the stream which runs northwards to join the Yeo. There is a riding stables here, with facilities for disabled riders. The pub, the Carpenter's Arms, provides an excellent meal.

Leigh

The 15th century church of St. Andrew stands in a quiet setting and has a battlemented tower, pinnacles and gargoyles. Nearby, an ancient cross on a 15th century shaft is one of two others existing in the village. It is for its mediaeval Miz-Maze that Leigh is particularly noted, however, though all that remains today are a few green banks in a field.

Dorset possesses at least two other mazes and probably many more besides, though none are preserved. Arthur Mee tells us that the maze here at Leigh was once of 'such cunning design that it took a man a long time to thread it'. Centuries old, it was said to have been maintained from generation to generation 'as zealously as the white horses all cut in the hills'. It was apparently repaired once a year by the young men of the village, and originally consisted of a hexagonal ditch 26 yards across, with a circular platform in the middle.

# LILLINGTON

Off the Dorchester to Sherborne road, just north of the turning to Leigh, one comes, by way of a quiet leafy lane, to the tiny village of Lillington. A surprisingly isolated village it is too, considering its proximity to Sherborne; as one soon discovers on descending Lillington Hill past the Old Rectory.

The church, dedicated to St. Martin, stands on rising ground, adjacent to an old barn with collar beam timbers dating from c. 1600. An embattled, six-pinnacled tower surmounts the church, its corners ornamented with large griffins alternating with smaller gargoyles. The churchyard affords fine views looking across open country above Beer Hackett, towards the valley of the Wriggle.

Old Barn Lillington

Having acquired the key as directed, one discovers a narrow white-washed interior, attractive in its simplicity, with no division between chancel and nave. Features of interest include the plaster barrel roof, a 16th century font, and many monuments to the Gollop family. One reads, too, of a vast mansion once existing, with dairies and fishponds, and housing many famous guests. Taken down in 1800, only sections of the foundations now remain.

Another point worth noting is the church's connection with Sir Walter Raleigh. In February 1589 or thereabouts, he had secretly married Elizabeth Throckmorton, one of Queen Elizabeth I's maids of honour. Their eldest son, Damarei, born 29th March 1592, died in infancy, but the following year, another son, Walter, was born. Baptised at Lillington on the 1st November

Lillington church

1593, the register in which the event was recorded has long since been lost. The entry – 'Walter, son of S.W. Rahley' – can still be seen in the Bishop's Transcripts, however, a copy of which hangs on the south wall of the church.

It is considered possible that the baptism took place in this out-of-the-way village rather than in Sherborne Abbey, because it was still necessary for Sir Walter (a favourite of the Queen) to maintain a measure of discretion, following her displeasure at the discovery of his marriage. Young Walter grew up a headstrong youth and – much to the grief of his parents – was killed in 1617 whilst leading an attack in Guiana. Further information concerns another son of Sir Walter, who by his father's Will was made his beneficiary. Yet another son, Carew, was born early in 1605 when Sir Walter was imprisoned in the tower.

A limestone quarry of some importance once existed near to the village.

# LITTLE BREDY

Cut off from the outside world, Little Bredy lies in a tranquil valley of wooded downs. From the road above, a path gives access to a church half hidden by beech trees. Dedicated to St. Michael and All Angels, it dates mostly from 1850, though some older parts remain. Rebuilt by Robert Williams of Bridehead to the design of Benjamin Ferrey, it possesses an unusual looking spire.

The names 'Bridehead' and 'Little Bredy' derive from a celtic word meaning 'to boil or throb'. They refer to the little stream which has risen here for more than 2,000 years. Our modern pronunciation of 'Bredy' is said to be misleading; people with their roots in the valley still say 'Briddy' which is apparently nearer the sound of the original name. The earliest reference was in 987 when the already established Saxon manor of Brydian was given by the Earl of Cornwall to the newly-founded Abbey of Cerne. It was mentioned in the Domesday Book 100 years later as having enough land for 850 sheep.

Below the church, a notice on a gate indicates that the public may walk through the grounds of Bridehead House (c. 1830) as far as the notice marked 'Private', provided one leaves no litter or feeds the ducks. Extensive lawns with trees and shrubs border a large artifical lake, the source of the Bride. This is a peaceful spot and ideal for a picnic, the only sounds to be heard the waterfall cascading over the rocks, or the occasional plop as a fish rises for air or a moorhen dives beneath the surface of the lake.

Beyond another gate lies the model village with its line of picturesque cottages, their gardens a blaze of colour in Summer time. Access is by means of bridges over the stream.

Little Bredy

# LODERS

This is an attractive village with a well-kept church standing in a walled churchyard. Overlooking the church and situated on the site of an old priory is 18th century Loders Court, from 1921 to 1961 the home of the late Colonel Sir Edward and Lady Le Breton. A bell cast in 1641 is a memorial to the couple who were regular worshippers. It weighs a ton and hung in the tower for nearly 300 years. In 1927, to save it from being melted down, it was placed where it now stands.

There is much of interest in the church. Saxon work on the north wall of the nave and chancel is evidence of the existence of an earlier ecclesiastical building on the site. Recorded history begins early in the 12th century, at which time the manor belonged to one, Richard de Redvers, Earl of Devon, who had connections with the Abbey of St. Mercy de Montburg in Normandy. When the Abbey ran into financial difficulties, he presented it with the manor of Loders. The small contingent of French monks from Montburg who took possession of the village at this time, brought with them, it is believed, the art of cider-making. They grew their apples in what was known as Priory Orchard lying to the southwest of the church, over what was once the railway line.

An arrangement of three small doorways grouped in the north wall of the nave is probably unique. The top doorway opened into the rood-loft; a second, at the top of a staircase, still gives access to the pulpit which is built into the wall; the third opens into both. To quote Arthur Mee, 'the preacher would have to pop into one doorway and out of another before he faced his congregation'.

A number of intriguing discoveries have been made in the church, including a large recess at the east end of the chancel wall which, when excavated, proved to be an Easter Sepulchre. Another find was a skeleton so decayed that only the lower leg bones were intact. The remains were placed in a lead casket, along with a copy of the 'Bridport News' and a box of contemporary coins, and re-buried. A 13th century Calvary group was also dug up from beneath the pavement of the chapel.

Another fascinating find was the lid of a stone coffin which came to light when digging took place under the floor of the nave. Believed to be the tombstone of a French monk who became Prior of Loders in 1363, it is to be seen to the north of the chancel, bearing the inscription: 'Here lies Dom John Sampson, sometimes Vicar of this place'. The door of the spiral staircase of the tower, with Fleur de Lis, is dated 1250 and believed to be one of the oldest in the country.

Finally, the church registers date from 1636 and contain records of 4,004 burials in the churchyard. With the previous burials of which there are no records, it is estimated that the churchyard holds the remains of some 10,000 bodies. The registers also disclose that in 1883 the population of Loders was

1,105, which figure has today been reduced to a mere 500.

The Old Vicarage, partly 16th century, has been replaced by one of more recent date, and nearby stands Loders Hall. The village, which lies within the borough of Bridport, contains a number of houses dating from the 17th century.

Loders

# LONG BURTON

Six miles out of Sherborne lies the village of Long Burton, spread out, as its name suggests, on either side of the Roman Road which runs from Dorchester to the Abbey town. Its church of St. James the Great possesses a 13th century squat tower; in spite of having been heightened in the 15th century with parapet and gargoyles, it appears to have sunk into the high gabled roof.

'Curse not the King, noe, not in thy thought' runs the inscription (taken from Ecclesiastes) under the Royal Arms of 1662 situated over the south doorway. Equally striking is the quotation: 'Feare thou the Lord and the King and medelle not with them that are given to change' (Pro 24,21) – no doubt dating from the Civil War, and a plea by Charles I for support.

Moving on to the north chapel, one finds two large canopied monuments, colourful and recently restored. One comprises two recumbent figures – a man in armour with his head on a book, and his wife in ruff, gown and cloak – and is to the memory of Sir Henry and Lady Winston of Standish in Gloucestershire, who lived during the reign of Elizabeth I. Their daughter, Eleanor Fitzjames of nearby Leweston, requested that monuments to her parents' memory be installed at Longburton, her husband's parish, a similar request having been turned down by Standish. An alabaster figure of Sir Henry's father, Thomas Winston, would seem to have been removed from Standish at the time of the dispute. Standish apparently relented at a later date, though the monuments erected were of inferior quality. The second monument commemorates Sir John Fitzjames and his wife, Joan, parents of Leweston Fitzjames, who married Eleanor.

LONG BURTON CHURCH

There is a connection here with Sir Winston Churchill. Eleanor's sister, Sarah, married John Churchill of Glanvilles Wooton, the couple becoming grandparents of the notable John Churchill, Duke of Marlborough, of Queen Anne's reign – ancestor to Sir Winston Churchill. A third monument is to the memory of the parents of Leweston Fitzjames who were bequeathed the property at Leweston (farther along the road towards Sherborne) in 1584. Below the slab on which they lie is a large collection of stone bones, a spade, a pickaxe and one or two skulls.

In the north aisle vestry, the Long Burton Turret-clock is a relic of the late 17th century and was made by Thomas Bartholomew, a Sherborne clock-maker. It was repaired and restored in 1972, entries in the Churchwardens'. Accounts referring to payments for 'keeping ye clock'. Bartholomew was also responsible for the one (still in working order) at nearby Yetminster. Clocks of this type would have needed to be wound every day or on alternate days, no doubt with outsize keys.

From the churchyard there is a pleasant view across fields, looking towards a lovely, rambling, partly 15th, partly late-16th century house known as West Hall. Set a quarter-of-a-mile back from the main road, it lies close to a small tributary of the Caundle Brook, the villages of this name being not far distant. Though not open to the public, there is a right-of-way for pedestrians along the driveway and past the house. Immediately ahead lies Folke with its little church of St. Lawrence; built in 1628, it underwent restoration around 1875. Nearby stands the old brown-stoned gabled manor house of Fontleroi, parts of which date from the 15th century.

# MAIDEN NEWTON

This village of some three hundred houses stands at the junction of the river Hooke and the Frome. Set amidst rolling downs and farmland, it was once a busy market town but now possesses a somewhat sleepy air. A nearby mill with arches over the stream was used in the manufacture of carpets until closure during the 1970s.

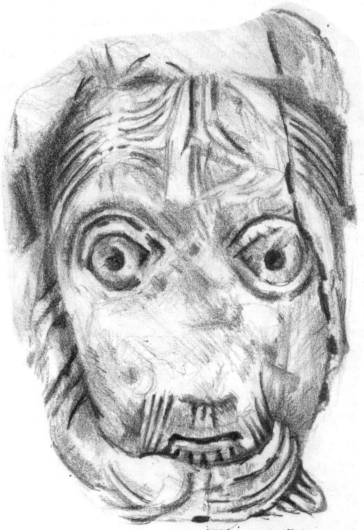

man holding moustache
maiden Newton church

The church of St. Mary dates from Norman times and is well worth a visit. Its Norman door, believed to be still hanging on its original hinges, is of particular interest, for it is said to be one of the oldest in the country. Appearing never to have had lock or latch, there are grooves in the stonework on either side which would originally have held a wooden bar for locking.

This church also has the distinction of bearing bullet holes from both Cromwellian times and of later date. The former were reputedly occasioned by Cromwell's men firing at the building when Royalists were hiding inside; the latter during the second World War when a bullet fired from an aircraft penetrated a window. The bullets themselves have recently disappeared from the holes in the ancient door.

To the south of the churchyard stands the imposing former rectory, now Maiden Newton House, where Charles I stayed during the Civil War. The cross in the centre of the village is of the 15th century.

Stone carving Maiden Newton church.

maiden Newton house.

# MAPPOWDER

Overlooking the ridge of Bulbarrow lies Mappowder a tranquil village far removed from the noise of traffic and the hurly-burly of the outside world. It is one of four situated to the west of Bulbarrow, the others being Stoke Wake, Hazelbury Bryan and Woolland.

The written history of Mappowder commences with the Domesday record of A.D. 1086, the name being originally Mapeldre, a form of Anglo-Saxon Mapulda(or), meaning a maple-tree, another variation being Mapoudre. During the reign of King John (1199 - 1216), there was an important royal lodge built at Mappowder, the remains of which were later to be incorporated into the structure of the Tudor manor house, Mappowder Court – home of the well-known local family, the Cokers. Built of local rubble, with Ham stone window frames and dressings, this building now goes by the name of Place Farm.

Place Farm Mappowder

Reference to the Cokers, who took their name from East Coker in Somerset, occurs as early as the reign of Henry I (1100-35). In 1422, a Coker was appointed Sheriff of Somerset and Dorset, and in later years the family played an important part in the Civil War, fighting on the side of Cromwell and the Commonwealth. A Coker too, Thomas by name, was rector of the church for no less than fifty-seven years. The family lived at Mappowder Court until 1745, after which it was purchased by the Honourable John Spencer, whose son – also John – inherited the property a year later on the death of his father at the early age of 38. Interestingly, this gentleman was created Earl Spencer in 1765, from whom is directly descended H.R.H. Diana, Princess of Wales.

Another point of interest concerns Mappowder's connection with Theo-

*Mappowder.*

dore Francis Powys, the well-known fiction writer. One of eleven children of an Evangelical clergyman, Theodore was born in 1875 and attended Dorchester Grammar School (though several of his brothers were educated at Sherborne and Corpus Christi College). He later lived in Suffolk, where it is said that he 'attempted disastrously to be a farmer'. Retiring from writing in 1933, he eventually settled in Dorset, coming to live at Mappowder and taking up residence in the cottage with diamond-paned windows (Newleaze Lodge) situated at the entrance to the churchyard.

Here at Mappowder, Theodore, though married, lived the life of a hermit. He died in November 1953 at the age of 77 years and is buried in the churchyard, along with his wife, Violet Rosalie. Pointed out to me in the churchyard was a tree planted in memory of Theodore's sister, and I am told that interest in the writer is still maintained through a Powys society which meets regularly in the village.

The church of SS. Peter and Paul is neat and tidy in appearance, both out-side and in. Outside it is adorned with the usual gargoyles and a flying buttress; inside the 15th century windows of clear glass give a light, airy aspect to the building. There is a modern chancel and a Norman font, and earliest records show William de Lenttom as rector in the year 1251, though the original date of the church is unknown.

Particularly noteworthy is a small military effigy about eighteen inches in length, set in a recess in the south wall. There has been much speculation over this effigy. It is believed to be the figure of a knight who died on crusade, though his name and date of death are not known. Was his heart alone brought back for burial? and is it just his heart that is buried here? are the questions posed. (It has been suggested that he is holding his heart in his hands).

Two sculptured heads appear on either side of the recess, believed to be an old piscina. They would seem to have been carved at dates about 200 years apart and are believed to have been taken from the old corbel table which would have extended around the chancel of the 12th century church. They were probably placed in their present position at the restoration. The tower and arcade of the south aisle are mid-15th century and there are the remains of steps to the rood-loft which are most likely of the same date. The ornately carved corbel at the head of the eastern respond of the chancel would have supported one end of the rood-loft when it existed.

To the rear of the church exists a large old building, formerly the rectory. In the wall dividing it from the churchyard may be seen a bricked-in arched doorway which at one time provided access for the parson.

A long, narrow, triangular-shaped parish of 1,900 acres, Mappowder now unites with the neighbouring parishes of Hazelbury Bryan, Stoke Wake and Fifehead Nevill, to form a team ministry.

# MARNHULL

This village lies scattered amongst the little hills overlooking **Blackmore Vale**, and is the 'Marlott' of Hardy's 'Tess'. It possesses a number of stone houses ranging from mediaeval to modern Georgian, along with cottages and farms. A Tudor-style manor house (Nash Court) was given to Katherine Parr, wife of Henry VIII, who lived to be his widow. There is believed to have been a settlement here for centuries before the Romans came, excavations having revealed evidence of habitation from the Iron Age.

The church of St. Gregory possesses a splendid 15th century tower, imposing buttresses, and an 18th century parapet and pinnacles. It is a landmark for miles around. Inside, the 15th century, almost flat roof of the nave consists of carved panels, each one different. A new wooden ceiling at the eastern end, replacing an Elizabethan lath and plaster one, obscures the top of the wall-painting over the chancel. This Queen Anne fresco having the Lord's Prayer inscribed on it, is interesting; for in one corner, large black lettering shows through – the Commandments from Elizabethan times.

Three effigies, a rafter roof in the north aisle said to be of Irish Oak, a pulpit of Marnhull stone, and a number of 17th century hatchments are other features of this interesting church. Of particular note is a stone bench inside the tower porch – a relic of the days before the 13th and 14th centuries when churches contained no pews. These stone seats were used by the elderly and infirm, and this gave rise to the saying, 'Let the weakest go to the wall'.

A very old and rare oak portable offertory collection box may be seen in the Hussey chapel. Of the six bells which the church possesses, the fifth – which has been rung for six hundred years – is very valuable.

Marnhull

# MELBURY BUBB

Arrived at by way of narrow, winding roads apparently leading nowhere, this village is tiny and comprises a little church backed by thickly-wooded Bubb Down, a few cottages and a farm or two.

Font melbury Bubb

Font melbury Bubb

Dedicated to St. Mary, the font is a curiosity. A very early example of Dorset art of the first half of the 11th century, it is believed to be part of a sculptured Anglo-Saxon cross or column, the lower end having been hollowed out to form the basin. Around its sides, intertwined with tendrils, are representations of a lion, a wolf, a horse and a stag. Why was not the other end of the column used, is the question posed; for the creatures are the wrong way up!

One explanation is that the sculpture was intended to show 'the overthrow of cruelty by the gospel of love' – or it could have been purely accidental. In his 'Dorset', Arthur Mee puts a different interpretation upon the carvings, describing them as a 'bold and handsome circle of hounds chasing deer, with wild beasts preying on each other'.

An Elizabethan manor house adjacent to the church is now a farm. This is an exceedingly peaceful and unfrequented spot.

Melbury Bubb

# MELBURY OSMOND

Lying north of Evershot and just south of the Somerset border, Melbury Osmund is a striking village situated on a southward-facing incline with a stream and ford at the bottom. The name 'Melbury' is believed to be made up of two Saxon words; 'Mel'. common to other west country place names, may be translated 'many coloured', 'Bury' means an earthwork. The whole is thought to refer to the pattern of the countryside, particularly the trees.

Descending the hill, one passes the Old Rectory and the 17th century Post House, as well as a number of fine thatched cottages. At the top of the hill stands an aisle-less church dedicated to St. Osmond, Bishop of Salisbury from 1078 to 1099. Considered to be the third ecclesiastical building to exist on the site, it dates from 1745; in which year, according to a memorial to Mrs. Susanna Strangways Horner on the south side of the chancel wall, 'this Parish Church, being ruinous, was wholly taken down and rebuilt on the same Foundation . . . by her generosity'. It was during the later restoration of 1888 that an old two-decker pulpit surmounted by a sounding-board was reduced to its present proportions, the same fate overtaking the five-foot high box-pews. Choir stalls and a vestry were added at this time.

Mask of Dorset Ooser
Melbury Osmond

Features of particular note are the mediaeval head set into the vestry wall, and the cherub's head and 'Abraham's ram caught in the thicket' in the walls of the chancel. A booklet written by a previous incumbent gives a fascinating insight into the past life of church and village. Rector from 1855-1910 he was the last to visit his parishioners on horseback. He acted as village dentist too, extractions taking place in what is now the rectory dining-room.

Here again there are associations with Thomas Hardy. His mother, Elizabeth Swetman by name, was a native of the village who, after spending some time in London, moved to the locality of Stinsford. Here she met her husband-to-be and though her father strongly disapproved of the young man from Affpuddle, they were married in Melbury Osmond Church. Their fifth child was Jemima who became Thomas Hardy's mother.

The village has connections with the Dorset 'Ooser', an alarming-looking creature wearing a bull's mask which appeared at the various assemblages held in a number of Dorset villages during the Christmas holiday period. Melbury Osmund's survived until the beginning of the present century.

# MINTERNE MAGNA

The 'Great Hintock' of Hardy's novels, this village of mellowed stone cottages lies in a dip between High Stoy and Dogbury Hills. Entirely unspoilt, it has retained its old world atmosphere.

The little church abutting on the road is crowded with memorials, one of these being to the Napier family – well-known in Dorset. Sir Nathaniel's monument is large and he lies adjacent to his father, Sir Robert, who held the position of Chief Baron of the Exchequer for Ireland. He built an almshouse in Dorchester which he called Napper's Mite. Other monuments include one to Charles Churchill, son of an earlier Winston Churchill, and brother of the Duke of Marlborough who fought at Blenheim and died in 1714 aged 56. The Digby family is also represented.

Minterne Magna

High trees hide the manor house, the home of Lord Digby, with its lovely park and woodland garden of trees and flowering shrubs. The gardens are open to the public from April to October and are well worth a visit.

# NETHERBURY

Close to the source of the river Brit lies Beaminster, with Netherbury situated 1½ miles to the south. The latter lies off the beaten track and is approached by way of a narrow lane from the Bridport/Beaminster road. Here at Netherbury where the river flows beneath a bridge, a good view may be had of the church standing on rising ground at the north end of the village. Flax mills in the valley once supplied the Bridport fishing-net industry, one such mill still surviving at nearby Oxbridge.

Netherbury's church is 14th/15th century and contains the More monument in alabaster. It dates from around 1480 and is badly damaged. The More family came from Melplash Court, a Tudor building situated about two miles south-east of the village. Here during the reign of Henry VIII lived Sir Thomas More, a relative of the more famous Sir Thomas. He was Sheriff of Dorset and would seem to have been somewhat eccentric. On one occasion he threw open the doors of Dorchester prison and let out all the inmates, including pickpockets, highwaymen and sheep-stealers.

No one was amused except the Sheriff and he not for long, so the story goes. He begged pardon of the King which was granted on condition that he handed over one of his richly-dowered daughters to Lord Paulet. This he did and with her went Melplash Court as part of her inheritance. Thus Melplash passed into the hands of the Paulets who were Marquises of Winchester.

Other points of interest in Netherbury church are the Elizabethan pulpit of inlaid oak and the large square font of the late 12th century. There is a drawing of this font in Dorchester Museum, which shows it without its base and standing on higher pillars. A clock in the church tower may date from as early as 1700 and is apparently still in good working order.

In the reign of King Edgar, Netherbury was designated Netherburie and at the time of the Domesday Book was known as Niderberie. It was once one of the largest parishes in Dorset for until 1847 it included Melplash, and up to 1849 Beaminster, with Mapperton attached. It is worth noting the fluctuating population of the village – 1,152 in 1811, 2,162 in 1841, decreasing to 782 in 1951.

# NETHER CERNE

This is a small village in a delightful setting of fine rolling downland. A flint-and-stone-banded manor house, once the Parsonage, stands in close proximity to the church of All Saints.

Now in the care of the Redundant Churches Fund, Nether Cerne's church originally formed part of the Abbey of Cerne which came into being during the 9th century. No traces remain of the Saxon church which might once have existed on the site. The present building was originally a chapelry of the Abbey and was served by the Benedictine monks until the Dissolution of the monasteries; after which, it became a perpetual curacy in the charge of the incumbents of Frampton, Godmanstone and Cerne Abbas. There is Victorian restoration inside, and the font has been described as shaped like a bell-flower.

It was in 1968, due to the very small population of the parish, that the little church was made redundant – becoming finally so, somewhat sadly one feels, in December 1971.

All Saints Nether Cerne

# PIDDLEHINTON

This grey stone village possesses a massive 15th century church. Low and square, it is mostly Perpendicular in style, with large gargoyles projecting from the four corners of the tower. Set in a hollow and surrounded by a fair-sized graveyard, it contains many intriguing features.

In the chancel, an amusing portrait on brass is of an earlier rector, Thomas Browne (1590-1617). He is depicted wearing a tall hat and carrying a walking stick. Also in the chancel is a small Priest's Door and two hagioscopes or squints, along with memorials to other early rectors. A sedilla of the 15th century comprising three stone seats would have provided cramped accommodation for priest, deacon and sub-deacon.

Of particular interest is the Turret Clock at the rear of the church, very rare and discovered only as recently as 1975 in the room under the bell chamber of the tower. Up to this time it had been looked upon as just a heap of old iron bars. Made by Lawrence Boyce of Puddletown in 1730 and recently restored, this remarkable clock needed to be wound every day, for which service the clerk received the sum of 6/- per annum. Having no face, the time was produced by means of a bell, the time-keeping needing to be adjusted now and again to keep in line with the sundial.

The history of Piddlehinton is recorded from the year 1068 when William the Conqueror over-ran Dorset and gave the land to his half-brother, Robert of Mortain, as a reward for his generosity in providing 200 ships to enable him to

Piddlehinton.

cross the English Channel. The village was once known as Hyne-Puddle, meaning the 'Marsh of the Monks', later becoming Honey Puddle. In 1972 it was joined with the other valley parishes of Piddletrenthide, Plush and Alton St. Pancras into a single ministry.

Lantern Cottage stands in front of the church, with the Post Office adjacent and the village hall nearby. The Old Rectory and some lovely thatched properties grace the gradually ascending road – all combining to present a very pleasing aspect to this most attractive village. Four pig farms with 60,000 pigs apiece exist in the vicinity, however, so nowadays it is a little less peaceful than it once was.

# PIDDLETRENTHIDE

Flowing from the middle of Dorset down through the villages to which it gives its name is the river Piddle – called 'Pidele' in the Domesday Book. It runs out into its own estuary between Wareham and Poole Harbour and seven villages take their names from it.

Piddletrenthide was once known, along with Piddlehinton, as 'Long Piddle', it being unclear where one village ends and the other begins. It straggles along its green valley for a considerable distance, and contains a manor house erected towards the end of the 18th century and incorporating parts of an earlier building. In 1812 this manor was leased to the Bridge family, notable jewellers and silversmiths, who made the Crown of State for Queen Victoria – still worn by the sovereign on occasions such as the State Opening of Parliament. A third storey was added, and in 1848 John Bridge provided the school building, the gates of which were said to have surrounded the tomb of Mary, Queen of Scots in Westminster Abbey.

In William the Conqueror's time, three mills existed at Piddletrenthide, the village being assessed for thirty hides, a measure of land varying from 60/100 acres – a large amount at that time. 'Trente' meaning 'thirty', this was how the village got its name. In 1654, a fire may have been the reason for the villagers moving away from the lanes near the church and stringing themselves out along the main road. Until the 1950s, the principal owner was Winchester College.

The church of All Saints has been described as one of Dorset's finest. It is mostly 15th century, with contrasts of grey and dark yellow sandstone, and a porch of stone and flint. Its tall tower is striking and possesses a number of alarming gargoyles. There is much of interest inside the church including a font with a base of Ham Hill stone, dating from the 14th century. There are various monuments to the Bridge family and others.

# PLUSH

A narrow hill out of Piddletrenthide, steep, winding and overhung with trees, brings one within a mile or so to a small hamlet nestling in a quiet valley surrounded by thickly wooded hills. The road through Plush is narrow – almost too narrow for cars – and centrally situated is the well-known pub, the 'Brace of Pheasants'. Amongst the whitewashed cottages, curiously-named 'Prisoner's

Plush

Cottage' catches the eye.

To reach the church of St John the Baptist, it is necessary to scale the hill; for it stands above the village, well hidden behind a number of large yew trees and cedars. An air of decay hovers over this building at present, and it is no surprise to see the notice 'Church locked, building dangerous, keep out'. A further warning inside the churchyard states that crash helmets should be worn.

The church was originally designed by Benjamin Ferrey in 1848 and altered in 1883. It is now longer than it once was. Inside is said to exist 'a dark Victorian Gothic tunnel with parapet above the buttressed nave'.

Adjacent stands a manor house with Victorian restoration.

# PORTESHAM

Nestling beneath the shadow of Portesham Hill, this village possesses many charming houses and cottages. Its church of St. Peter is 15th century, the limestone exterior appearing almost white in the sunshine. Typically Dorset in design, its tower is well-built. The remains of another tower are to be seen on its northern side.

The interior is Victorian and there is an unusual epitaph on the south wall, referring to one, Mary Weare:

> 'Whose good meek heart did alway shun
> Such things as ought not to be
> done'

Outside, back-to-back with it, is a table tomb with another epitaph:

> 'William Weare lies here in dust,
> As thou and I and all men must,
> Once plundered by Sabean force,
> Some call it war but other worse'.

Thus the two inscriptions to this 17th century couple are divided by the church wall.

Portesham Church.

72

On top of the hill out of the village stands the famous Hardy Monument on Black Down (pronounced Black'on). It is a landmark from all around, with a view stretching from White Nothe to Golden Cap, Weymouth and Portland lying between. Built in 1844 to commemorate Nelson's flag captain at Trafalgar (not, of course, Dorset's Thomas Hardy, though one might be forgiven for thinking so), it is also an excellent sea-mark. The bracken and heather-covered hill forms part of Wareham Forest.

A mile east of Portesham, grey-stoned Waddon Manor (c.1700), backed by a steep green hill, looks out across Waddon Vale. It is all that remains of a former building of the reign of William III or Queen Anne, burnt down in 1704. A farm for nearly 200 years, it became privately owned in 1928.

# POWERSTOCK

Said to be one of the most attractive villages of the downs to the north-east of Bridport, Powerstock (or Poorstock, as it was once known) lies south-west of Toller Porcorum and Toller Fratrum, and north of Nettlecombe and Uploders. Situated amid hills and valleys and quietly-flowing streams, it stands on

Stone carving Elizabeth of
Hungary. Powerstock church.

74

Stone Carving
Goool King Wenceslas
Powerstock church

varying levels at the foot of the Iron Age hill-fort of Eggardon, a portion of which comes within the parish boundary.

The church is set high on a hill, and from its walled churchyard one looks down upon a variety of cottages, thatched and otherwise, scattered over hill and dale. A large, derelict building of Victorian/Gothic style at the bottom of the incline, originally the schoolhouse, was considered too small for the purpose at the time of the Education Act of 1870. It continued in use as the teacher's house, however, until the occurrence of a near-disaster. Due to softening of the stone, a bathroom wall collapsed, almost causing the death of the teacher's daughter. After this, the building no longer functioned as a residence and in 1968 it was sold. It was subsequently taken over as a store-house and is still used for this purpose today.

The church is mid-12th century, its most striking feature being its superb – though not very symmetrical – semi-circular Norman chancel arch, built of local stone and heavily ornamented. Saxon stone carvings and a double squint (or hagioscope) are also worthy of note; as is the 13th century font, at one time relegated to the churchyard. Considerable restoration took place in the Victorian era, at which time the galleries were removed and the chancel rebuilt. All the stained glass dates from the last half of the 19th century.

Norman chancel arch Powerstock.

A rare feature in the churchyard is the 13th century dole table standing on the left-hand side of the path leading from the main entrance. From this ancient table charitable doles of bread would have been distributed to the poor and needy.

Also of interest in the north-east corner of the churchyard is the grave of Kenneth Allsop, writer and broadcaster. He lived in the adjacent hamlet of West Milton, and from 1970 until his death in 1973, owned Milton Mill, now the home of the High Sheriff of Dorset.

There is no church nowadays at West Milton, though at the top of an incline may be seen an ancient tower standing within an oblong grassy plot, along with some old tombs and monuments. Once forming part of a chapel-of-ease believed to have been dedicated to St. Michael, the remainder of the building fell into decay. It was demolished shortly after 1873, the stone being used in the building of Powerstock's new school. The lancet-headed window originally situated in the east end of the chapel was also incorporated, together with a 15th century two-light window and a 12th century door.

By way of a replacement, another church was built in 1873 at the other end of the hamlet, from stone taken from the Nettlecombe quarries. This new church survived only about one hundred years, being declared redundant in 1974 and demolished three years later.

The name of Powerstock in one form or another is believed to have existed before the Norman Conquest. On a hill-top to the south-west of the village, a green mound is known as Powerstock Castle, an earthwork believed to be considerably earlier than the 11th or 12th centuries. It is said to be all that remains of Athelstan's Castle which, according to tradition, once guarded the valley. A Norman motte and a bailey fortress, together with a hunting lodge of King John, are known to have once existed here.

From 1857, a railway line joined Powerstock to Bridport and Maiden Newton and proved a lifeline to the village in times of severe winter weather. It existed for over one hundred years until 1975, when it was closed by British Rail and the track lifted. The station was sold and converted for private use.

Powerstock

78

Powerstock.

# PUDDLETOWN

This village is the 'Weatherbury' of Hardy's 'Far from the Madding Crowd'. Earliest records show that in Saxon times it belonged to Earl Harold; it later passed into the possession of the Earl of Dorset, and after the Norman Conquest reverted to the Crown. Its highlight is undoubtedly its magnificent, mainly 15th century church with turreted tower – a portion of the latter being the oldest part of the present building.

On entering the church, one is immediately struck by the seating, which consists entirely of box-pews. The large gallery to the rear was erected in 1635 and contains choir-stalls indented with numerous initials, presumably of choristers. According to a list of choir members, numbers stood at 26 in the 1920s. Beneath the gallery are suspended several canvas fire-buckets dated 1805, at that time the property of the Sun Insurance Company of Bath. Unless so displayed, fire insurance would not have been granted.

Other features of this fascinating church include the pulpit and prayer-desk combined, made in 1635; the cover over the font which was placed there to comply with a direction of Archbishop Laud; and the steps to the rood-loft which are in a very good state of preservation. A ring in the middle of the south door is thought to have been a Sanctuary Ring.

In the Athelhampton Chantry on the right of the chancel are brasses and effigies of the Martyns, an old Dorset family. Also to be seen are the mutilated effigies of a Knight and his Lady, along with tombs dating from the 13th and 14th centuries.

# PUNCKNOWLE

Rambling and secluded, the pretty village of Puncknowle (pronounced 'Punnell') is backed by a ridge of downs and possesses many attractive thatched cottages. The Crown Inn stands opposite the Norman church of St Mary with its squat tower. Norman in origin, access to the church is by a flight of steps and a lychgate.

Inside, one finds a number of monuments to the Napier, Napper or Naper family. One, having initials only, commemorates Sir Robert Napier who died in 1700. The inscription runs thus:

> 'Reader, when as thou has done all thou can'st thou are but an unprofitable servant. Therfore this marble affords no roome for fulsome flattery or vaine praise Sr. R.N.'

The north aisle was added in 1891, though the nave is modern. In the south aisle is the Bexington Chapel, used as a vestry since 1966, and containing an undated memorial to William Napier.

manor House Puncknowle.

In 1440, the old village of Bexington which dated from Saxon times had, together with its church of St. Giles, been razed to the ground during a raid by the French. On the 8th September 1451, at the request and by the consent of the patrons, the Bishop declared the parishes of Bexington and Puncknoll to be one; it being further decreed that the rector of Puncknoll should celebrate in the chancel of Bexington once a week and on St. Giles Day. The chapel was erected for the use of the villagers, and later passed into the possession of Bindon Abbey. It remained thus until the dissolution of the monasteries. In 1660 it was restored, later being transferred to Puncknowle where it became known as the Bexington Aisle or Chapel.

Outside the church, an ancient-looking moss-covered stone slab close to the west wall is believed to be a 14th century coffin lid. To the rear of the churchyard, an iron gate leads to a partially turreted manor house which has been described as 'the most compact and charming of all Dorset manors – a tiny gabled Jacobean house of grey weathered stone, exquisitely proportioned.' Yet another gate affords a glimpse of extensive velvet lawns.

With its chestnut trees, low-sweeping branches, and the incessant cawing of rooks, this churchyard is a peaceful spot.

# PURSE CAUNDLE

The Caundle villages of Bishop's, Marsh, Purse, and Stourton lie amid rich pasture and scattered woodland in the Blackmore Vale between Sherborne and Stalbridge. Purse Caundle, the most northerly of the four, is a peaceful spot, its 15th century and lovely many-gabled Elizabethan manor house dating from c. 1470 being well worth a visit. The manor house with its variations of stonework and wall textures is said to be one of the most enchanting in Dorset. The present owners are Mr. and Mrs. M.R.A. de Pelley, who bought the house in 1984.

The history of the original manor starts in 1055, at which time Purse the Elder built cottages for 175 serf families and called the village after himself. In 1241 it was known as 'Purscaundel', and it is probable that there once existed, on the site of the present manor, two previous manors or hunting lodges. King John, who frequently hunted in Dorset, would very likely have visited here.

There is a record too of a John Aleyn who held an ancient form of tenure directly from Henry III. This man is said to have lived at the manor or lodge in 1269 'to keep or lodge the King's sick or injured hounds at the King's cost when the Lord King hunted game in Blakemore'. A subsequent owner described it as 'a royal dog hospital'.

For over 300 years, Purse Caundle Manor has remained in its present form, only a few minor alterations, mostly to the interior, having been carried out. In 1959 a large part of the roof collapsed and it was after restoration that the house was opened to the public. The 16th century south front facade is in the shape of the Royal 'E'.

The church, rebuilt around 1480, stands in the centre of the village and contains a fine canopied table tomb of William Long, a former owner of the manor. The effigies of himself and his wife were probably destroyed during Cromwellian times. A floor-slab in the chancel is to the memory of Nathaniel Highmore, M.D. (1613-1685), a distinguished physician and son of a former rector. There are a number of other floor-slabs and brasses of former owners of the manor, and a chained Bible is particularly noteworthy.

Purse Caundle manor

# RYME INTRINSECA

More picturesque than the village itself, its name (sometimes spelt 'Intrinsica') means 'a place on the inner rim or edge of a ridge' (Intrinseca' – 'inside', 'Rima' – old English for border or rim). Thus, we have a settlement within a sheltered place. 'Intrinseca' was apparently not added until the 15th century when it was necessary to distinguish between In-Ryme and Out-Ryme. At that time, the lord of the manor of Ryme also owned such widespread properties as Hallynges Manor at Long Bredy and part of the manor at Langton Herring, as well as land in Hermitage, Hammoon and Sturminster Newton. These lands, known collectively as Ryme Extrinseca (outside), were eventually sold off, leaving only Ryme Instrinseca remaining.

Ryme Intrinsica

The church of St. Hypolite, with its two lancet windows and green and purple cathedral glass, was included in the List of Buildings of Special Architectural or Historic interest in the 1961 nationwide survey. It possesses an unusual dedication; only one other church in the country, St. Ippolytes near Hitchin, Hertfordshire, is dedicated to St. Hypolite – though there are a number of similar dedications in France. Born in 170 A.D., this little-known saint was the gaoler in charge of St. Lawrence who was roasted on a gridiron. Apparently the example set by the saint so impressed Hypolite that he became

a convert to the Christian faith. He died in Sardinia c. 235 and his feast day is
13th August.

Ryme Intrinsica

# SANDFORD ORCAS

Situated four miles north of Sherborne, Sandford Orcas lies in peaceful surroundings amongst hills. A border village, it belonged to Somerset until 1896, of which county it is more characteristic. Three streams rise here, forded in Saxon times over sand, from which the first half of the name is said to derive; the second being attributed to a former owner, a Norman by the name of Orescuilz. At its northern end exists a Tudor manor house, standing close to the churchyard wall.

Sandford Orcas manor

This charming Dorset house has survived practically unaltered and possesses virtually all its original windows, doorcases, fireplaces and staircases. It was built in the 1550s by Edward Noyle at the age of 21. (He later became the King's Escheator for Somerset and Sheriff of Somerset and Dorset in 1492). Apart from several short letterings, it has been occupied by only three families; firstly the Knoyles, then the Hutchings who bequeathed it to a kinsman, Sir Hubert Medlycott. The Medlycotts have owned it for the past 250 years, the same family also having connections with Edmondsham House, near Cranborne. Sir Mervyn Medlycott is the present owner.

Thirty-five ghosts were said to haunt this house in recent years; it was reputedly 'the most haunted house in Britain'. The story appeared on television and T.V. cameramen spent a night there in the hope of a sighting. With the expiration of that particular tenancy, however, the 'ghosts' mysteriously disappeared, never to return.

Ghosts or no ghosts, the visitor to Sandford Orcas Manor will not go away disappointed. A small manor house similar to many to be found in England during Tudor times, it is a gem. Built on the foundations of a mediaeval stone manor, the main fronts and dressings are of Ham Hill ashlar, the lesser fronts of grey rubble limestone possibly quarried at nearby Marston Magna. Some sections of the former building survive, including walling in the central courtyard and other areas; also a window situated near the north-west corner of the house facing the church – a tiny squint carved out of a single block of stone.

Features of the interior include the Great Hall with its enormous splay of windows filled with heraldic glass and rising to the first floor; the Solar Stairs leading to the Great Chamber; and two newel (spiral) staircases (rarely found in 16th century domestic buildings in Dorset) which survive unaltered. It is understood that Sandford Orcas is unique in that it is the only house in the country having original staircases of this type; it is certainly unique in that one is clockwise, the other anti-clockwise. Also remarkable are the original oak-studded doors of which ten survive complete with locks and keys, the latter not easily transportable in the pocket due to size.

Interestingly, Sandford Orcas is one of the earliest Tudor houses in Britain to possess straight tops to the windows. It is also the only Tudor house in the country with a gatehouse attached to the side of the main front. Enormous window displays such as the one in the Great Hall were to become fashionable in large houses such as Hardwick fifty to sixty years later. Of these Bacon quaintly said: 'Faire Houses, so full of Glasse, that one cannot tell where to become, to be out of the Sunne, or cold'.

The nearby church of St. Nicholas, of Ham Hill stone, possesses a 15th century tower and chancel. Traces of 14th century work are to be seen in chancel and nave; a 13th century font resembling an upturned Canterbury Bell possesses an oak scroll cover of the 1600s. Late Victorian restoration of 1871 has left its mark.

In the small south chapel exist monuments to the Hutchings family, but of particular interest is one to William Knoyle dated 1607. He wears armour and his two wives are surrounded by their children, those of the first lying stiff and dead on a skull. An inscription states that he married 'fillip, daughter of Robert Morgane by whom hee had yssve 4 children and bee dead.'

# STURMINSTER NEWTON

The small, north Dorset market town of Sturminster Newton is the one referred to as 'Stourcastle' in 'Tess of the D'Urbervilles'. Its fine church, originally built in the Perpendicular style, underwent extensive alteration during the 18th century so that only the outline of the original remains. Inside exists a memorial to William Barnes, one of Dorset's three 19th century poets.

Two other poets have connections with 'Stur', as it is known. Rabin Hill was a tailor by profession and lived at the 'Hive' near the mill. From him Dorset's more famous poet, Thomas Hardy, rented the grey manor house known as 'Riverside' which stood adjacent. Hardy lived here from 1875 to 1878, during which time he wrote 'The Return of the Native'. The house, now privately owned, may be seen across the far side of the big meadow.

A grey 15th century bridge over the river Stour has moulded coping and six pointed arches. On it exists one of those strange plaques threatening deportation for life to anyone found guilty of damaging or defacing it.

The 17th, partly 18th century mill is L-shaped and stands 260 yards upstream. It has been restored and is in full working order with a tenant miller in charge. Part of it now doubles as a shop where booklets and picture postcards may be purchased. The picturesque building in its tranquil setting is a scene popular with artists and is one of three mills in the vicinity – the other two being Fiddleford and Cutt Mill, neither of which are now in use.

Sturminster was originally a royal estate owned by King Alfred, and there were probably mills here during the Saxon period, forerunners of the present ones. Records suggest that these were wooden and remained so until the 16th century. The Sturminster mill is one of four watermills listed in the Domesday Survey of 1086, of which three were granted to Glastonbury Abbey by King Edgar in 968. At the time of the Survey, the mill at Sturminster was assessed at 40/- a year, the last account rendered to the Rivers estate for thatching bearing date 1862.

The north wing of the mill, which is of brick, could have been added in the middle of the 18th century. The traditional water wheel was replaced by the greater efficiency of a turbine in 1904 and is still in good working order. Based upon the principle of a horizontal rather than a verticle wheel, it is somewhat similar to early Greek and Norse mills still to be seen in the Scottish isles. It is also said to resemble some early Saxon ones.

Even in the driest weather the Stour can be relied upon to provide a sufficient volume of water to drive the mill machinery. A weir upstream retains the water at a high level, and this is controlled by a series of hatches alongside the mill building. Sturminster Newton is fortunate to have retained its mill in good working order.

Stourminster Newton Mill

# SWYRE

This is a small, grey village, somewhat reminiscent of Cornwall, lying in a valley down by the Chesil Beach. Buildings old and new line one side of the main street, at the far end of which stands the Manor Farm and the church. A good meal may be had at the Bull Inn.

The Bull Inn Swyre

In days gone by, Dorset possessed its share of strange beliefs, and Swyre, along with certain other villages, had its 'Black Dog' legend. These animals were usually considered to be unlucky and sightings were said to have been reported in various locations. A creature known as the 'Jumping Black Dog' was reputed to haunt the road between Puncknowle and Swyre.

The church of Holy Trinity is a plain, unadorned little building dating from 1505; though only tower and chancel arch remain from this period, it having been largely rebuilt in 1863. Its list of rectors dates back to John De Candel of 1297, no previous records surviving. The Dorset historian, John Hutchins, is amongst their number, being instituted to the living in 1729. He is noted as having repaired the chancel at his own expense.

Some early 16th century brasses commemorate the Russell family of Berwick House a mile to the north. John Russell rose from farmer's son to courtier in a somewhat unusual manner. In 1506, a ship with the daughter of the King and Queen of Castille aboard, together with her husband, Philip, Archduke of Austria, had been forced to put into Weymouth due to bad weather. The royal couple were entertained by Sir John Trenchard at Wolfeton House, near Dorchester. John Russell, because he could speak Spanish, was called upon to act as interpreter. He accompanied the party to the Court of

Henry VII at Windsor where he came to the notice of the King. He was subsequently established as a courtier and rose during the next thirty years to positions of high standing. His successors became Dukes of Bedford from 1614 onwards.

Another notable of the village was Colonel Shrapnel (1761-1842), the inventor of the deadly shell.

# SYMONDSBURY

Situated in a wooden hollow between Bridport and Chideock, this lovely village of yellow sandstone lies in a wooden hollow at the foot of Colmers Hill, facing towards Eype Down and Golden Cap. In days gone by it was reputed to possess, in common with certain other Dorset villages, a curing well which was believed to be beneficial to sore eyes – a belief based, no doubt, on the sulphur contained in the water. To obtain maximum relief, the water had to be taken early in the morning as soon as the sun's rays touched it.

A cruciform, 14th century church dedicated to St. John Baptist occupies the site of an earlier building. There is a plastered waggon roof over the nave, an 18th century pulpit, and Georgian three-sided Communion rails. Choir stalls of fairly recent date have carvings of flowers, birds and animals. Banished to the back of the organ in the north transport, boards bearing the Commandments, Creed and Lord's Prayer now occupy the south transept. There are some fine yew trees in the churchyard.

Opposite the church a gabled, yellow-stoned school house is of date 1868. There are many pleasant cottages and much thatch is in evidence. The 18th century former rectory is now a farm.

Symondsbury school house.

# TINCLETON

This is another village having a link with Thomas Hardy. Diggory Ven, the Reddleman, came to live at one of Tincleton's dairyhouses after his marriage to Thomasin Yeobright. As to how it got its name, nobody seems to know, except that 'ton' means a farm.

Valued at twenty shillings in the Domesday Book, Tincleton comprises a cluster of houses, a church with one or two larger houses nearby, and an Elizabethan Manor called Clyffe House. Built in the 19th century, the latter was the birthplace of one of the members of Parliament expelled by Pride's Purge. Clement Walter was his name and he was eventually banished to the tower for airing his views on the corruption of parliamentary government – where he died.

The lovely old church dedicated to St. John the Evangelist stands in a tranquil churchyard. It has a nave, chancel and porch dating from 1851. The striking reredos is of 1889.

Near to the village lies a picturesque bridge over the fast-flowing river Frome. A footpath follows the meandering stream across the water-meadows.

# TOLLER FRATRUM

This tiny settlement stands on a hillside overlooking the point where the Hooke meets the Frome. It is not directly accessible by car from neighbouring Toller Porcorum; though on foot it would probably be possible to follow the stream or the railway line running between the two villages.

The name means 'a stream in a valley of the Brethren', and refers to the Knights Hospitallers of St. John of Jerusalem who had associations with Forde Abbey. Here at Toller existed their mansion, their refectory, and their storehouses. After the Dissolution, the mansion was rebuilt on the ancient foundations as a secular dwelling-place by a prominent Royalist, Sir Thomas Fulford.

The manor house is today known as Little Toller Farm. ('Little' Toller as opposed to Great Toller, or Toller Porcorum). Said to be one of Dorset's loveliest houses, it is a fine specimen of domestic architecture of the early part of the 17th century. Slated and of weathered grey masonry, it features arch-headed Tudor windows, twisted stone chimneys and pinnacles bearing heraldic symbols. Of particular interest is the prominently-sited chained monkey holding a mirror, along with a winged griffin, and a lion with a shield bearing the Royal Arms.

At right-angles to the house, a long thatched building which is believed to have been the refectory of the Knights Hospitallers, bears an appropriate carving in stone of a man eating a loaf. In more recent times, this barn housed twelve cart-horses.

To the side of the barn a little 19th century church, with a Norman chancel and nave, occupies a tiny churchyard. Possessing neither tower nor spire but only a bell-turret, it is one of only four ecclesiastical buildings in this country dedicated to Basil the Great, one of the most important saints in the churches of the East. Inside exists a tub-shaped font said to be very early Norman or even Saxon, decorated with a number of crudely-carved figures.

The farm has been in the ownership of the same family since the late 1800s. During the war, a bomb dropped nearby but did little damage, though a cow narrowly escaped death. Even this remote spot was not exempt!

11ᵗʰ century Font Toller Fratrum church

mary magdalene washing feet of Christ. Toller Fratrum

# TOLLER PORCORUM

This village of 200 inhabitants (including the hamlets of neighbouring Upper and Lower Kingcombe), lies in an attractive, shallow valley. 'Toller' was the original name of the river Hooke on which the village stands; it was probably altered to 'Hooke' by the Staffords, Lords of Hooke, in the 15th century. In the Middle Ages, the village was known as Swynestolre (a Saxonised version of the name) or Hogstolre. For it was a place notable for the feeding of swine in the oak woods.

There is another explanation, however. The name could derive from the wild boar hunted by kings in Powerstock Forest which in those days encroached on the village. There are few pigs to be seen nowadays, though deer roam freely, as do foxes, badgers and hares. The village is mentioned in the Domesday Book, and is known to have been farmed from earliest times. It bears evidence of mediaeval strip cultivation.

The church of St. Andrew and St. Peter comes within the Beaminster area team ministry. It stands on an elevation between railway and stream, at the centre of the village. Parish registers go back to 1615 and record incumbents from 1235. A Victorian iron staircase leads to the bell-ringers gallery, and a spiral stone stair gives access to the bell-chamber at the top of the tower. There have been alterations over the years; the high box pews were removed during restoration work in 1894, as was the gallery, attained formerly by means of an outside wooden staircase. The font is said to be part of a Roman altar.

A recent collapse of a length of wall bounding the churchyard above School Lane led to an interesting discovery. Stones about 2½ feet x 2 were brought to light (they may be seen at the east entrance), which would seem to confirm a belief that at one time this churchyard may have been a Llan or Lan, a word meaning 'holy'. Llans, created by Celts in pre-Roman times, were sites roughly circular in shape marked out by a ring of standing stones. A number of such sites seem to have existed in the West Country and were taken over by the first Christians, who built their churches within them.

Close to the church lie Manor House and a former vicarage, St. Peter House. Adjacent to 'The Old Swan' stands another former vicarage, Toller House – the second of three to have existed.

The approach to the village is under the old railway arch. A single track railway built in 1857 formerly ran between Maiden Newton and Bridport, passing through Toller. Until May 1975, a single coach with a diesel engine traversed the line and provided a convenient means of surveying this beautiful piece of Dorset countryside.

# TRENT

This is an extensive village, isolated and approached by narrow roads with high banks surmounted by trees. Attractive with its hamstone houses and cottages, it lies between Yeovil and Sherborne, and is a border village. In common with other such villages, it underwent transference between Dorset and Somerset on more than one occasion, the last being in 1896 when it reverted to Dorset.

Trent has altered little since the time when Charles II fled to it disguised as a servant after the Battle of Worcester. To the accompaniment of triumphantly pealing bells proclaiming his defeat, he took refuge in a priest's hole in Trent Manor, a £1,000 reward on his head and death for anyone hiding him.

The 14th century church dedicated to St. Andrew contains much of interest. At the entrance to the churchyard, the large building now in use as a private dwelling was built c.1400 by John Franks, Master of the Rolls and a native of Trent. Originally the home of the chantry priest, no sign of the chantry chapel now remains.

The stone spire atop the church tower is unusual for Dorset, though similar to many existing in Warwickshire and North Oxfordshire. It is said to be the work of the Augustinian Priory of Studley in Warwickshire, to which a part of the manor of Trent belonged from 1250 until the Reformation.

In the porch, a quaint old notice requests that 'All persons . . . take off pattens and clogs before entering'. Inside the church, an ornate carved pulpit dating from 1600 was brought over from Holland by a former rector. Another unusual feature is the wording over the archway of the Manor chapel in the north transept. In looking-glass writing, it reads: 'All flesh is grass and the glory of it as the floure of the feilde'. Its purpose, one gathers, was to remind the young ladies of the Manor of their vanity, when they looked in their mirrors instead of listening to the sermon.

Also of interest are the pre-Reformation (early 1500s) pews carved with symbols in such a way that four of them put together form the prayer, 'AVE MARIA GRATIA PLENA DOMINUS TECUM AMEN'. It is said that when Cromwells' soldiers were approaching Trent, the villagers thought the church would be burnt down if the Latin prayer were discovered. So they unscrewed the pews and mixed them up, and they remained thus until quite recently when one group was returned to its original position. The only other set of similar pews existing in Dorset is at Bradford Abbas.

Apart from its Royal visitor, Trent has another and more recent claim to fame. In 1962 the village became the retirement home of Lord Fisher of Lambeth (1887-1972), and Lady Fisher, when they were offered the use of Trent Rectory for their lifetime. The Archbishop frequently conducted services at Trent and remained there until his death, when he was interred in a magnificent Victorian vault. Re-discovered in 1970, the latter had been intended for a former rector, the Rev. W.H. Turner (1835-70), but was never used. The stone slab commemorating the ninety-ninth Archbishop of Canterbury may be seen close to a cross with a circular base and modern steps situated in the churchyard.

Before leaving the church it is worth noting the glass in the east window which is Swiss and German of the 16/1700s. A property of this glass, the secret of which has now been lost, is that when the sun shines through, the colours are not reflected on the floor.

Of the remainder of the village, the Manor house, invisible from the road, stands next to the church. Farther on lie the Rose and Crown Inn, and four almshouses built by Mary Turner, wife of the former rector.

Trent

# UP CERNE

This charming little village – hamlet might be a better description – lies along the banks of the river Cerne, along with Nether Cerne and Cerne Abbas. It comprises a manor house, a church, and some pretty cottages.

The manor house is gabled and of stone, built in the 17th century by Sir Robert Mellor. The north wing was added later, and there is an 18th century south front.

In close proximity within the drive stands a Norman church of unknown dedication. The early 16th century chancel was rebuilt in 1870, and has an 18th century plaster ceiling. Nave and tower are also largely rebuilt.

Though the main road passes close by, Up Cerne lies hidden and remote.

Up Cerne manor house

Up Cerne

# UPWEY

Situated at the source of the five-mile river known as the Wey, this one-time beauty spot for visitors to Weymouth retains its rural quality and charm. It is still untroubled by crowds, but was not always so apparently. At the turn of the century, it was said to be 'rather too much over-run with trippers brought in the brake which ran constantly in summer time from Weymouth, to be attractive to those who love peace and quietness when they are in the country'.

This was Thomas Hardy's setting for parts of his novel, 'The Trumpet Major'. It is bordered on its north side by forty or so terraced cottages enjoying uninterrupted views across open fields. Elwell Street joins the old borough of Bincome on the east to that of Elwell on the west. The latter is particularly picturesque. In a narrow valley beneath hills and sheltered by a thick screen of trees stands the 13th century church of St. Laurence, together with an old mill beside the stream and the famous wishing well.

The late 15th early 16th century church is dedicated to St. Laurence who died a martyr's death and was burnt on a grid-iron. The tower is tall, with gargoyles and pinnacles. A small piece of wall is all that remains of the church which formerly existed. Just above the porch is a water-spouting gargoyle with a boy astride a wolf holding its mouth open. Passing through the iron-studded, 500 year old door, wall frescoes are to be seen to left and right of the porch. Those to the west are quotations from the Book of Proverbs (Chapter 24, 20-22); the lettering in the bottom right-hand corner is damaged and indecipherable, however.

Of particular interest are the painted Tudor Roses between the arches of the arcade; these have recently been renewed after rediscovery beneath old wall-paint and inch-thick plaster. Three wooden plaques on the walls are believed to have been taken from the pedestal of a Jacobean pulpit, and worth noting is the paler colour of the bottom 10 inches or so of the pews. This was a result of a torrential storm which occurred in July 1955, when water swept down the valley, flooding into the church.

An ancient monument and the largest natural spring in the British Isles, Upwey Wishing Well is said to be the only authentic well in existence on the south coast. King George III often stayed at Weymouth, finding relaxation from the severe mental illness to which he was subject. During his visits, he, made frequent trips to the Wishing Well in order to partake of the clear, fresh water from the spring. It is believed that the golden cup from which he drank is the one now used at the Ascot races.

A century ago 'English's Wishing Well Tea-Gardens' existed beside the well. So many visitors came to the Well during the summer months that two of the older village inhabitants were appointed to sit by the well as 'glass-givers'. These elderly ladies would tell people how to wish, in exchange for which

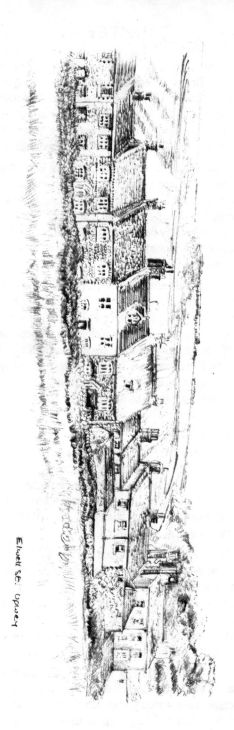

Elwell St. Upwey

104

service they received a small tip. A see-saw and two swings were provided for the entertainment of the village children, who would carry water from the Well to their cottages.

Previous to 1920, a small boy earned seven pence a week for daily transportation of two large cans of water, hung on a yoke, to Teacher's Cottage lying between the Well and the church. The girls would bring their hoops with them when they came to collect water; standing inside the hoops, they would raise them on either side and hold a pail in each hand. The hoops prevented the pails banging against the sides of their legs as they walked, and they were able to convey the water safely home without spillage.

Today there is a small café and gift shop near the Wishing Well. It is said there are few wells in existence clearer or fuller than this one.

At the east end of the village, the white chalk lane (the old Roman road), rises to the summit of Ridgeway Hill. Legend has it that at times of national crisis, Roman armies appear, marching above Weymouth.

# WHITCHURCH CANONICORUM

Four miles or so within the Dorset/Devon border one comes upon a signpost indicating 'WHITCHURCH CANONICORUM 1½ miles'. Situated within the Marshwood Vale, this parish was at one time one of the most extensive in England, including within its bounds Charmouth and Chideock. Today, it still covers a large area, extending from the edge of Charmouth to Golden Cap, and from the coast several miles inland. It contains the daughter church of Stanton St. Gabriel, and no less than 56 farms, it is said, some of which date from the 17th century.

The village is a peaceful spot with little in the way of modern buildings. It is dominated by the perpendicular, buttressed tower of the church of St. Wite (or St. Candida) and Holy Cross. This church claims to have been founded by Alfred the Great who, in his will dated 890, bequeathed Whitchurch (then known as Hwitancircian) to his youngest son, Ethelwald. Whether its name derives from the fact that it was built of stone rather than of wood (the reason for the many 'Whitchurches' to be found in this country) or because of its connections with St. Wita, is not known.

Be that as it may, for many centuries Whitchurch Canonicorum was a place of pilgrimage, for within its church existed, and still exists, the shrine of St. Wite. Of all the shrines once to be found in this country, only two still remain intact – this one and the more famous shrine in Westminster Abbey, that of Edward the Confessor.

No one can say for certain who St. Wite was; as a historian of Victorian times once observed, her identity appears to have been surrounded 'by a curious haze'. Originally known as Wita or Wite, the name was altered to Candida towards the end of the Middle Ages (St. Candida's Day is 3rd October). It is thought probable, however, that St. Wite was an Anglo-Saxon hermit who devoted her life to good causes, including helping the sick.

So much for St. Wite, but what of her shrine? Built into the wall of the north transept, this unusual feature of the church dates from the early 13th century and is of local golden stone. The upper portion consists of a Purbeck marble tomb chest; underneath, three large oval openings are almost big enough for a person to climb inside. Within these would have been placed the injured and diseased limbs of pilgrims who had come for healing; for the chest above contained, and still contains, the remains of St. Wite.

The relics were discovered in April 1900. During the preceding winter, movement of the walls of the north transepts had caused an ancient, 13th century crack in the tomb chest to widen. When the broken piece was removed the following Spring, a lead casket was discovered lying on its side in the interior. 2' 5" x 8" high, it bore a Latin inscription which translated is, 'HERE REST THE RELICS OF ST. WITE'. The contents appeared undisturbed and were believed to be the bones of a small woman aged about 40; they were returned to the tomb chest where they remain to this day. Thus Whitchurch Canonicorum is the only parish church in England to have a shrine containing the remains of its patron saint.

Some say that St. Wite lived near a well which still exists in the hamlet of Morcombelake. For centuries it was known as St. Wite's Well and the idea seems feasible; for hermitages were usually positioned close to fresh water. In mediaeval times, pilgrims would visit the well, the waters of which were believed to be a cure for sore eyes, and most effective when the sun's rays lit upon them. Surprisingly, the well retained this reputation even up to the 1930s.

Many footpaths and old tracks exist in the Marshwood Vale, and they still lead to the church, it is said. Visitors to the shrine today will find its floor covered with petitions placed there by those who seek healing for themselves, their relatives or friends.

Tomb of St Wite Whitchurch Canonicorum

# WINTERBOURNE STEEPLETON

Through this little village, one of the South Winterborne group, the road winds between trees, and a stream flows past thatched, flint-built cottages in a peaceful, picturesque setting. A lovely manor house, completed in 1870, is a registered retirement home, and close to an ancient church the stream runs under the road.

St. Michael and All Angels derives from a Saxon church of the first half of the 11th century. It is an unusual and interesting building. The stone steeple topping the low tower is considered to be a later addition; the nave is Norman with original doorways, the windows 15th century. At the west end is a white-painted minstrel's gallery of 1708. A blocked-up, 12th century arch in the north wall at one time gave access to a 15th century chapel; demolished in the 17th century, the site of the chapel is now occupied by a late 18th century vault of the Lambert family. Three layers of plaster on the north wall of the nave – pale green over white, with pink showing through – point to the presence of a wall fresco beneath of considerable size. This became damaged at a time when the value of such wall-paintings was not recognised. A portion of lettering is visible.

One of this church's most intriguing features is the stone angel bound with chains, incorporated into an outside wall of the nave about a foot above the ground. Some consider it to be the Archangel Michael to whom the church is dedicated, others an angel cast out of Heaven. Dating from at least the 11th or 12th centuries, it is believed to be pre-Conquest and an outstanding example of Saxon sculpture. It has been suggested that at one time it was one of a pair set on either side of the road, moved to its present position probably before the 18th century. More likely, however, it was originally situated inside the church over the chancel arch.*

Since the village is mentioned in the Domesday Book, its name would seem to derive from the steep hills which surround it, rather than from the steepled church. In Mill Lane adjacent to the church existed a watermill and the miller's cottage, and in a small cottage beside the road once resided the village carpenter. The Old Manor Cottage dating from the 16th century and occupying the site of an earlier rectory is the Old Rectory of 1850.

It is interesting to note that some of the older buildings have their backs to the present road. The original road ran further to the south.

*A recent visit to Winterbourne Steepleton revealed the 'Flying Angel' to be no longer in situ. The reason? Experts from London have reported it to be in a state of deterioration due to exposure to the elements. It has therefore been taken away for cleaning, and a faculty obtained for it to be set up within the chancel, thus preserving it for future generations.

Winterbourne Steepleton

# WOOLLAND

Time seems to have stood still in this corner of North Dorset, lying beneath Bulbarrow Hill on the edge of the glorious Blackmore Vale. Woolland has no shops, and even neighbouring Ibberton possesses only a post office. The nearest links with civilization would seem to be Childe Okeford three miles to the north-east, and Hazelbury Bryan in the other direction.

Opposite the church, behind iron railings, stands The Old Schoolhouse, erected in the last century and used as a school up to the 1940s. Original oak beams, wooden Gothic-type doors and glorious views through latticed windows across the Vale are features of this fascinating building. Two texts, painted in black lettering, remain on the walls of the former schoolroom; the one over the fireplace reads 'My little children, love one another', the other, 'Keep ye discipline in peace'. Two spacious old buildings lie to the rear in a courtyard backed by thickly wooded slopes. One is the carter's stables, originally the estate yard of the Mansion House which existed at the east end of the church. The Schoolhouse was occupied by the head gardener, whilst the schoolmistress lived in the village. An underground passage is said to connect church and school.

The earliest mention of Woolland was in a charter of King Athelstan, AD 939, to the abbey of Middleton, by which he gave 'Five hides in Wonlonde'. In Henry VIII's reign the village went to William Thornhull, an ancient family of the Blackmore Vale, with whom it remained until 1770; after which, most of the Manor was sold to John Gannet of Blandford, whose grandson, John Fever, built the Mansion House. Later purchased by Montague Williams who made a number of improvements, it was demolished in the 1960s, only the stable building remaining.

The church was erected in 1856 and replaced an old private chapel designed by Gilbert Scott, pulled down the previous year. Said to be one of Scott's favourites, it is comprised of a variety of stonework. The pulpit is a single block of Caen stone; carvings of leaves on the chancel columns depict every tree to be found in Woolland and surrounding districts. To the right of the east window, a stone replica of a robin's nest represents one left undisturbed by workmen constructing the chancel, until such time as the eggs had hatched out and the birds flown. In November 1986, the spire of the church was found to be in a dangerous condition and taken down at a cost of £5,000.

An enormous yew tree 60ft high x 53ft in diameter dominates the churchyard, believed to have grown into its present shape of several mighty trunks due to having been split. Partly held together by an iron brace, its measurement in 1871 was 23ft around the circumference, and more recently 31ft. It is said to be 1,000 years old, though a more cautious estimate is '17th century and probably before'.

The house to the west of the church (it has the reputation of being haunted) is known to some as 'The Rectory'. Built in the reign of Queen Elizabeth or James I as the Manor House, it was given as a dowry to Thornhull. Designed in the old style with living rooms and the fireplace of the Hall off to the right, the kitchen premises to the left, it is large, irregular and originally L-shaped. At some time in its history, twelve servants were employed. It is believed to have been connected to the adjacent chapel, or at least to have extended some way towards it, and an oast house was said to adjoin it to the south. At the time of the Blandford fire in the mid-18th century, it was enlarged to provide homes for the homeless.

All that remains of the Mansion House to the east of the church is the stable building, currently the home of the sculptress, Elisabeth Frink. A tragedy occurred here in recent years when the clock tower fell, killing the wife of a previous owner.

old Schoolhouse Woolland

111

# WORTH MATRAVERS

This attractive stone village, of which a prominent feature is the duck-pool, stands at the head of a long valley high above the sea. Its church dedicated to St Nicholas is one of the oldest in Dorset. Norman with traces of Saxon, the nave dates mainly from 1150, and there is a spectacular chancel arch of the 13th century. A Saxon doorway is blocked up within its 12th century walls. The windows are mostly small and high, for as Arthur Mee points out, the villagers being but a mile from the coast, they would live in fear of sea raiders.

Buried in the churchyard beside his wife lies Worth's most notable character, Benjamin Jesty of Downshay. The inscription on his tombstone tells of 'An upright and honest man, particularly noted for having been the first person (known) that introduced the Cow Pox by inoculation, and who, from his great strength of mind, made the experiment from the cow on his wife and two sons in the year 1774.'

At the ancient manor house known as Downshay lived the Maltravers family whose heirs were the Earls of Arundel. They gave their name not only to Worth, but to Langton and Lytchett Matravers as well.

A path down through the valley brings one to Winspit where the surrounding hills are full of quarries. Owned for generations by local families, they are today, like the Tilly Whim Caves at Swanage, merely a tourist attraction and no longer worked. Victims of an East Indiaman, wrecked at nearby Seacombe in 1786 with the loss of many lives, lie buried in the church.

village pond at Worth matravers

# WYNFORD EAGLE

This tiny village was once held by the post-Conquest baronetcy of Aquila (the Eagle) situated at Pevensey in Sussex, a Norman family taking its name from L'aigle in Normandy. Prior to 1096 according to the Domesday Book, it was held in demesne by William of Eu, who died after being blinded and mutilated for his part in the 1094 plot against William Rufus.

The church of St. Lawrence is of Ham Hill stone and dates from 1842. A larger one once occupied the water-meadows to the south, the foundations of which have recently been seen from the air. Of particular note is the tympanum set seven feet above ground level on the outside of the west wall, near the porch. Dating from the 12th century, it is believed to have once constituted the head of the doorway of the former building. The carved stone is intact and depicts lettering of date c.1096, similar to that of the Bayeux tapestry. In simple and shallow relief, two winged dragons face each other in angry confrontation, and there are twelve scratched imitation voussoirs. The wyverns are presumably intended to be decorative, and not a 'Good versus Evil' contest.

Further on in time, Wynford Eagle had connections with the ancient family of Sydenham, who came from the town of that name near Bridgwater in Somerset. Born in the manor house at Wynford Eagle in 1624, Thomas Sydenham became one of London's leading physicians. He commenced practising medicine at Westminster in 1655 and is notable for having introduced quinine as a cure for the plague. He played a prominent part in the Civil War, fighting on the side of the Parliamentarians.

12ᵗʰ century tympanum Wynford Eagle.

The Sydenham family owned the manor from 1551 to 1709, during which time they rebuilt it. From above the date '1630' on the central gable of this 17th century building an impressive eagle looks out over the rolling open countryside.

church Wynford Eagle.

# YETMINSTER

To the east of Ryme Intrinsica, and not more than a mile or two from the Somerset border, lies Yetminster, a fine village with golden mullion windows, both ancient and modern. It possesses many splendid, stone-built 17th century houses, amongst them 'Priors Cleve', the Old Library, the Old School and the Old Vicarage. A wall plaque on another commemorates a grammar school founded by Robert Boyle in 1691.

There are long houses here too, from the days when the family occupied one end of a building, farm animals the other. They have been preserved very much in their original shape. Pubs include the White Hart and, with the railway line running close to the village, the Railway Inn, a number of its windows boarded up. Beyond the church, a pleasant stroll across field paths affords extensive views across the downs.

A church is said to have existed at Yetminster for one thousand years or more, though very little has survived from early times. The Minster of St. Andrew, large and imposing, is Perpendicular and early English in style and dates from the 1400s. On top of the tower, a gilded weathercock is of the 18th century.

There is much of interest inside the church. Affixed to the west wall of the south aisle is the base of a 12th century Purbeck marble font; two alabaster cloaked figures standing in the east window of the north aisle are believed to be part of an ancient reredos. A 10th century cross on the north wall of the chancel is notable for its carved figure wearing a halo – a feature common in the north, though unique in the south-west. Amongst the monuments is a brass to Sir John Horsey, esquire to Henry VIII, buried here in 1531.

Several times a day the bells of the church chime the National Anthem. Installed to celebrate the Jubilee of Queen Victoria, they belong to a faceless, 300-year-old clock of 1682 made by Thomas Bartholomew, the Sherborne clockmaker who was responsible for the one in Long Burton church. Until 1986 when it became automatic, a team of village men climbed the fifty or so steps to the belfry daily, for the purpose of winding the three movements of this ancient time-piece and keeping the chimes going.

Yetminster is recorded in the Domesday Book as 'Estminstre', and in spite of the proximity of the railway line, is an impressive village.

carved pulpit. Yatminster